D1112014

The

XYZ

Factor

The XYZ *Factor*

The DoSomething.org Guide to Creating a Culture of Impact

NANCY LUBLIN & ALYSSA RUDERMAN

CHLOE LEE, COLLEEN WORMSLEY, FARAH SHEIKH,
HILARY GRIDLEY, JEFF BLADT, JOSH CUSANO,
JULIE LORCH, LIZ EDDY, MUNEER PANJWANI,
NAMITA MODY, SARAH PIPER-GOLDBERG

BenBella Books, Inc.
Dallas, Texas

Copyright © 2015 by Nancy Lublin and Alyssa Ruderman

All rights reserved. No part of this book may be used or reproduced in any manner whatsoever without written permission except in the case of brief quotations embodied in critical articles or reviews.

BenBella
BenBella Books, Inc.
10300 N. Central Expressway
Suite #530
Dallas, TX 75231
www.benbellabooks.com
Send feedback to feedback@benbellabooks.com

Printed in the United States of America
10 9 8 7 6 5 4 3 2 1

Library of Congress Cataloging-in-Publication Data:

The XYZ factor : the DoSomething.org guide to creating a culture of impact / DoSomething.org, Nancy Lublin, Alyssa Ruderman.
      pages cm
   Includes index.
   ISBN 978-1-941631-63-8 (trade cloth)
   1. Social responsibility of business. 2. Corporate culture. 3. Social change.
4. Social movements. I. Lublin, Nancy, 1971—II. Ruderman, Alyssa, 1988—
III. DoSomething.org.
   HD58.7.X99 2015
   658.4'08—dc23
                                 2014042907

Proofreading by Greg Teague, Jessika Rieck, and Clarissa Phillips
Text design by Kit Sweeney
Text composition by PerfecType, Nashville, TN
Cover design by Keri Goff
Jacket design by Sarah Dombrowsky
Printed by Lake Book Manufacturing

Distributed by Perseus Distribution
www.perseusdistribution.com

To place orders through Perseus Distribution:
Tel: (800) 343-4499
Fax: (800) 351-5073
E-mail: orderentry@perseusbooks.com

Significant discounts for bulk sales are available. Please contact Glenn Yeffeth at glenn@benbellabooks.com or (214) 750-3628.

To our friends and families . . . who'd better buy lots of copies.

CONTENTS

ACKNOWLEDGMENTS

There are a lot of people who fuel the work that we do day to day and the work we've done for this book, so here we go . . . we'd like to thank:

- Our board of directors: Larry Berg, Steve Buffone, Matt Diamond, John Faucher, Icema Gibbs, Reid Hoffman, Kim Kadlec, Raj Kapoor, Todor Tashev, and Darryl Wash
- Marlon, who keeps our office clean
- Varsano's, for keeping our stomachs full of chocolate-covered everything
- Whoever was responsible for Google Docs
- Toto for writing "Africa"
- Every other company for which any of us has worked. Some of them have taught us what not to do and some have helped us create this amazing culture.
- Former staff and interns, most noticeably George Weiner and Melanie Stevenson, who helped create this culture
- Crystal Ruth Bell, for sharing her gift of color with us. We'll continue to adventure, swipe right, and fight for the user in your name.

INTRODUCTION

THE XYZ FACTOR:
THE DOSOMETHING.ORG
GUIDE TO CREATING
A CULTURE OF IMPACT

THE XYZ FACTOR

You might have picked up this book because you wondered, "What exactly is the XYZ factor?" XYZ isn't a place or a company or an age. It's a mind-set—a new kind of culture where innovation, accessibility, and transparency are the norm. It's an environment created by behaviors and values, not a policy manual approved by external lawyers or board members. It indicates the successful coming together of three generations to produce boldly and efficiently.

Being a Millennial is limited to when you were born. Being XYZ is not. The XYZ Factor means adopting the principles of the Millennial generation to foster intergenerational productivity in a new kind of office culture. It means learning from how Gen Y operates and implementing those practices widely. There are plenty of Millennials who aren't XYZ and plenty of Gen Xers who are. Michael Bloomberg is XYZ, Seth Godin is XYZ, Michelle Obama is XYZ, this new Pope? We think he is pretty freakin' XYZ. We're writing this book because we think it's possible for *anyone* to be XYZ. It's a philosophy, not an age.

It could be at play in any company. Your company could be an XYZ company. Ours certainly didn't start out this way. We made it this way. We are an XYZ company because our organizational values reflect the generational makeup of our staff, our surroundings, and our target market.

THE GOAL OF THIS BOOK IS TO FOSTER ONE THING: PRODUCTIVITY.

This book is not a manifesto. This is a business book. An introduction to a new kind of office culture created by the arrival of the Millennial generation (our generation) to the workforce.

We are not interested in pitting our generation against yours. In fact, we get along with our parents so well that we want to live with them forever!

Think of this book as an instruction manual. We are quirky, complicated things. Proper care is required. Just like all our Ikea furniture, special little tools and tips are helpful in our assembly.

1. Chapter topics. We have written this book in the most simple, neat, easy-to-use format. Each chapter covers a different workplace topic, and the XYZ way to approach it.
2. Practical advice. In random spots, we have included "Tweetable Takeaways." These are little nuggets of brilliance in less than 140 characters. (FYI: that is the length of a tweet . . . and our attention span.) These points serve as a basic checklist of things you should do (or not do) to maximize harmony and productivity in your workplace.

WHY US? WHO ARE WE?

All the authors (and editors) of *The XYZ Factor* work together at DoSomething.org, the largest membership organization in the world for young people and social change. We work with millions of young people every day, helping them to do more volunteerism and community improvement projects. There are over 200 live campaigns at DoSomething .org from "PB Jam Slam" where teens donate jars of peanut butter to food pantries, to "Comeback Clothes" where members recycle stained and torn clothing to keep them out of landfills. These are big campaigns. In 2014, we collected over 100,000 jars of peanut butter and 421,000 pounds of clothing (!). Those are big numbers. These campaigns have a big impact on important causes. Big campaign numbers and a large membership also mean that we have tons of data and anecdotes at our fingertips, providing the inspiration for much of the basis of this book.

Our team at DoSomething.org is about 80 people (60 full-time and another 20 part-time). Of those 80 people, 13 of them are over age 30.

That's right; we work in an office of twentysomethings all day long . . . and many nights. We have practiced what we preach in these pages. And now we are preaching what we practice.

SEVEN SECRETS TO THE XYZ FACTOR

If you are going to manage us, partner with us, or work with us in any capacity, the first thing you need to do is "get" us. Notice we didn't say you need to "agree" with us or even "like" us. But it is absolutely a good idea to understand what makes us tick.

We are sharers. The following seven secrets are designed to give you that baseline understanding of what drives XYZ values.

1. WE VALUE CHOICE

You grew up with Skippy and Jif. The only big decision in those early peanut butter days was the shape of your sandwich. Did you eat it in halves? Triangles? Squares? Did you insist on the crust being removed? These were big decisions declared by empowered five-year-olds. You got to express a bit of a personal stamp on your sandwich, thanks to your mom and a knife.

Chemist Joseph Rosefield decided to introduce crushed peanuts into his butter and in 1973, Skippy "Super Chunk" was on the shelves. The advent of "crunchy" peanut butter was mind blowing. You'd go to a friend's house for lunch and discover if they were crunchy or smooth people. This was the Democrat/Republican divide of the elementary school set— friendships were lost and forged over peanut butter predilections.

Now, a visit to the peanut butter section of the grocery store is an adventure. The only way to describe the kind of choice available is to use the SAT word "plethora": organic, fat-free, all-natural, almond, private label, store brand, and our favorite: nut-free peanut butter.

We think this peanut butter panacea is normal. *Of course* there are lots of options. It is hard to imagine a world with just two kinds of peanut butter.

Or, think about TV. Watching TV used to mean ABC, CBS, or NBC. The TV was black and white, and you had to get up out of your chair to change the channels. The remote control (or "clicker") was bulky and loud, and it turned changing channels into a game-like activity . . . even though there were still only three options. The development of "cable" was like bringing fireworks to a town without electricity.

In 1981, you demanded "I want my MTV" in hopes of adding that station to your cable boxes. It was a brilliant campaign. More choice was preferable to fewer options—even if music television didn't appeal to you, you wanted to make that decision for yourself.

Today, there are literally thousands of cable channels. Since 1999 you can TiVo, adding another choice element to TV viewership: timing. And now there's DVR or Netflix or a dozen other contraptions and services to watch those programs when YOU want them, so even the notion of TV on your timeline is available via a rainbow of mediums. We watch only 79 percent of our TV live, compared to older generations that watch up to 92 percent of their programming unrecorded.

The punchline? Now that we have thousands of cable channels that can be viewed on multiple devices at any time of day, we aren't watching TV at all. We've turned instead to YouTube, where we have millions of options.

Or, consider college majors. Back when our parents went to college, there were a handful of "acceptable" majors. You studied History or English or maybe you were Pre-Med or Pre-Law. It was a path trodden by many.

In 2012, the Department of Education reported that there were 1,500 academic programs across the country. At places like the University of Michigan and Arizona State University, students choose from a menu of more than 250 majors. DePaul University in Chicago offers 24 more majors now than it did in 2002.

Want even more choice? Create your own thing. Make your own company. Your own YouTube channel. And, there is also the notion of "creating your own" major. Is "Medieval Hispanic Feminist Studies" your passion? Go for it.

Choice is the norm.

Limitless peanut butter, TV options, and college majors are the norm to us. Choice is not special, prized, or celebrated. Choice is expected.

It is this constant access to choice that leads us to feel bored or stymied. And so, we get antsy, moving around in search of more options. Our entire lives have been a page from "Goldilocks and the Three Bears"; we've always had the ability to move on from something when it wasn't the right fit. And why wouldn't we? If we didn't like grape jelly, we gave strawberry a try. If tap wasn't our thing, we were in a ballet class the next week. It's not about being spoiled or about having a lack of loyalty, it's about having so many options that it's normal to pick the one that fits best.

To be XYZ, your company needs to offer choices to employees. If choice doesn't exist, we're going to check out or just break the system and make our own option.

Where people used be happy to choose between two health care plans, a younger employee will be confused by the notion of "out of network" doctors. We ask, "Why should there be any limits on choosing a health provider?"

2. WE MOVE FAST

Organizing a club in college in the 1980s was a labor of love and commitment. To set up a singing group or an anti-apartheid group took a lot of time and patience. You had to ask for permission. It involved a lot of paperwork (handwriting or using a typewriter on a form you had to pick up in person during specific hours of the day). There was often a small processing fee. Assuming you received permission, you then typed up a flyer, found someone in your dorm with a printer, brought it to Kinko's to make copies (which could be picked up 2 hours later), postered the campus, and held the first meeting a week later.

Now, college students post something on Twitter or Facebook, friends "like" it or comment on it or RT it or share it . . . and ten minutes later, 30 friends are fired up about the new club. And, friends on five other campuses around the country are copying it.

Everything we've known is fast. Fast food. Next day test scores. Overnight shipping.

Slow-paced decision making alienates us.

We don't believe it actually takes you a couple of days to decide something—instead, when you say, "I need a few days to mull this over," it just feels like making the decision simply isn't a priority to you. To us, things that matter, happen quickly.

An XYZ Company doesn't take 18 months to greenlight a new idea. There aren't waitlists, lines, and protocols. XYZ companies deploy.

We don't wait in lines. We Open Table that reservation, StubHub that concert ticket (the night before), TaskRabbit that cronut, and SpeedPass that Disney ride.

Our attention span is shorter.

We fall in and out of love with Justin Bieber or the boy next door in the span of three weeks. Why? Because we don't drive to the record store to buy music; we download it in seconds. Because we don't flirt for weeks at the bus stop and then "date" the boy next door on a Friday night; we find him on Tinder, text with him and meet him for coffee. We don't talk on the phone, enjoying long conversations. We text. And we expect you to respond within minutes, using abbrvs because we don't have time to spell out or read full wrds.

These relationship examples are not coincidental: we form relationships very quickly. We meet a potential roommate on Craigslist and move in the next week. Yes, we move in with "strangers!" Basically, we move (in) quickly.

Or, think about the tail of a disaster. Even just 10 years ago, when a major disaster struck, it would remain front page news for weeks. For example, the tsunami in Indonesia in December 2004 captured headlines for nearly three weeks. But the December 2012 massacre of 26 young children at Sandy Hook School in Newtown was front page news for only five days.

Or, take entertainment. A film like *Lawrence of Arabia* would never be made today—he walked through the desert for eight minutes?! Today, a sitcom expects a laugh every 10–15 seconds. Twenty years ago, the gag cycle was 20–30 seconds.

Slow is synonymous with stupid.

Don't boil it on the stove if you can microwave it. Maybe you lament the loss of artistry and the lack of appreciation for patience, skill, etc.? Complain as much as you want. Fact is, we're going to use the microwave instead of sweating over the hot stove for half an hour.

"Slow talkers" are a thing. They are real and they make us nutty. Why use more words, more time, and more space if you can nail it in a quick bullet point, a blog post, or a tweet? Don't call us and talk our ear off, if you can text us and be done with it quickly.

3. WE'RE NOMADIC

A recent *Forbes* magazine headline announced: "Job hopping is the new normal." Headhunting firm Heidrick and Struggles says that a student graduating in the last three years will, on average, have sixteen different jobs by the time she or he is thirty-seven years old. At the University of Florida, 60 percent of students change their major by the end of their second year. We move around like we're running from the law! In fact, we're running from boredom, from working for the man, from the possibility of being stuck.

We don't just change jobs; we change apartments, houses, lovers, cities, states, and even countries faster than past generations. According to US Census data, people age 18–34 are the most mobile demographic. The report also states that the number of times a person moves is inversely proportional to their level of income. In other words, poor people move a lot . . . and that's us. Young people just starting out are going to bounce around before they find their perfect fit. We follow job opportunities, boyfriends, girlfriends, family, or just the desire to try a new city.

XYZ managers are aware that their employees are likely experiencing flux in their personal lives.

And we're not afraid to take big leaps either—30 percent of movers age 20–29 will move to a different country. In the 2010–11 academic year, 273,996 American students studied abroad for academic credit. Study abroad by American students has more than tripled over the past two decades. Nearly 110 million Americans currently own a passport; more than double the 48 million in circulation in 2000 and around fifteen times the 7 million in 1989. That's right; we see the scope of possibility as GLOBAL.

We are good at adapting to new things.

All of us have an older relative who still uses a typewriter or is afraid to install a garage door opener or insists that ice made in trays just tastes better than the stuff that comes from the machine. (And in fairness, it is possible that the ice does taste better from a tray. Coke in a glass bottle definitely tastes better!) However, it's also possible that the new way leads to new exciting flavors, efficiency of time and money, and other unpredictable possibilities. You just don't know unless you try, and we love trying new things.

"If it ain't broke, don't fix it" doesn't work anymore. XYZ companies try new things.

Because we have experienced so many changes—and change happening at an exponentially increasing rate—we are used to adapting to change. A new gadget doesn't sit in its box for weeks. Instead, we will tear into that new box and try it out. (Note: it's also entirely possible that in fifteen minutes we will declare this new gadget to be totally useless . . . but at least we tried it.)

4. MEASURABLE FEEDBACK

Our generation didn't grow up with Archie Bunkers and Howard Cunninghams. We had Danny Tanners (*Full House*) and Carl Winslows (*Family Matters*). We had parents, real and fictional, who were involved, vocal, and always told us when we were doing well (and less frequently when we weren't doing so well). Our fictional and non-fictional parents talk. A lot. They ask us questions. They text us. They show up in our Facebook feeds. In short, parents are all up in our business! In some way or another, subtle or overt, they're always telling us when they approve or disapprove.

From our real home to our second home . . . school. Schools give just as much—if not more—feedback than our parents. Parent–teacher conferences used to be once or twice a year. Now teachers send regular emails, work assignments and results are posted online, and there are even nursery schools that posts daily photos or have live webcams. We expect regular feedback.

Computers, the Internet, and cloud-based computing have made it possible to provide real-time feedback. You no longer wait for months for your test scores to arrive—you have a valuation in seconds. Your rank and how you compare to every slice of society is easy to discern (re: Twitter followers, Facebook friends, likes on Instagram, and Klout scores). Restaurant reviews don't come out annually in a printed book; they are posted in real-time online, for anyone to access. There is always a number, a percentile, an explanation—and that data is current to the minute. There are no more mysteries.

Annual performance reviews don't cut it anymore.

We expect quarterly feedback. Bosses, boyfriends, and karate instructors have to adapt: give us regular feedback! That means the performance review, the compliment, the next level belt—it needs to happen in a timely fashion or we check out.

We have been programmed to crave feedback. Most of us grew up in an environment that was teeming with high expectations coupled with constant evaluation. We're used to handing in multiple rough drafts of a paper before a final copy, gold star charts to mark our behavioral progress, and parents yelling from the sidelines. Regular evaluation is the norm from birth—where we apparently had an APGAR score, weight, and length measured—all of which were sent out in a proud email birth announcement, before we even left the hospital (because printed birth announcements are too slow for us).

XYZ companies create an avenue for constant and consistent feedback. Quarterly reviews over annual, weekly check-ins over monthly.

Spend time with us.

What it ultimately comes down to is that feeling valued is incredibly important to us. If we don't feel valued, then we start to question why we're doing what we're doing and we'll likely move on. We feel valued when you take the time to evaluate us. Regularly. We recognize that your time is valuable, so when you dedicate some of it to assessing our work, we know you're invested.

Where you spend your time is a proxy for what you care about. Spend in-person time with employees.

Constant feedback doesn't mean constant praise.

A lot has been written about this "everyone gets a trophy" thing—so much so that the idea is even known as a syndrome. Sure, giving out trophies for a game where no one keeps score is a little silly. Kids probably shouldn't be rewarded for just showing up. But we didn't create those policies and hand out those trophies—our parents did.

We'd be cool with constant feedback that isn't always positive— so long as it's given kindly. Maybe it's not a bad thing for everyone to be a bit kinder to each other. When you give feedback, you are not talking to a machine. You are talking to a person. Be kind. Smile. Ask if the feedback makes sense—and if not, don't just repeat things louder. Instead, try to more clearly explain the specific behavior and the people/things impacted as a result.

Give feedback out of kindness, an investment in someone improving, not out of anger and the need to punish.

Yeah, we understand that sometimes we mess up and your anger is warranted. That happens. But if you want us to improve at our job, think of your feedback as the means to a better end.

Be specific.

We've grown up in a numerical world. Computers and technology have allowed just about everything to be numbered, ordered, sorted, averaged, ranked, and so on. From ID numbers to rewards card numbers, to how many minutes it will take to drive from a specific address in West Hartford, Connecticut, to a specific address in Anchorage, Alaska, to social media followers—we've practically been walking around with a barcode on our butts since birth! Instead of sifting through a pile of "R" last names to search for us, we've been able to say, "My ID is 955763260." We don't say that we are a "B" student; we say our GPA is 3.58. And when we graduated high school, we knew that we were ranked 7th among our peers, or that we were in the top 10 percent of our class.

When we drop these numbers, we're not trying to have a pissing contest; this is just the language we speak. It's concise, it's specific, and everyone knows what it means to be 73 percent done. We believe life should come with a progress bar, letting us know how far we've come.

It's this kind of accuracy and specificity that we're used to; we expect feedback to be delivered the same way. Do we need to know that we got an 8.5/10 for this month's review? Probably not, but "average," "good," and "great" don't provide us with enough detail to grow. We have little patience for ambiguity. Don't tell us we're "Great!" Tell us the actual situation, the behavior we exhibited, and what positive impact we had on the outcome. Give us the deets!

We need feedback that is structured, productive, and actionable. We'd actually prefer to hear something specific, even if it's specifically what we did wrong. We should walk away from a check-in or review with an understanding of what we've kicked ass on, what we fell short on, and tangible next steps for improvement. Give us enough to work with.

5. DO OVERS

We spent hundreds of hours of our childhoods playing video games. In the realms of *Super Mario*, *Halo*, and *World of Warcraft*, there is always a reset button. By hitting it, you may lose a few points, or even have to start from scratch, but it's a chance to start again. That's right: we expect another turn.

Back in our Little League days, most of us didn't even know what it meant to "strike out." When we were up at bat, we could swing until our arms went numb and still never heard an ump yell, "You're outta here!" because we weren't out of there. We swung until we were tired of swinging and then we took our tired little arms and walked to first base.

Take the SAT as another example. When you took the exam, it was given twice a year in an overcrowded hall full of nervous sweaty teenagers who were pissed off at having to be awake at 9 A.M. on a Saturday morning. Your score on that one exam changed your life.

Today, if you score below the 1800 that your dream college requires (or if you're rich and just love taking tests), there's no need to worry. Just cough up the $50 registration fee and you can fill out those tiny bubbles as many times as it takes to get a score that feels right to you.

Or, think about something as simple as writing a letter or a paper for school. When you wrote a paper, you wrote one draft and maybe one final draft. You put your head down and got up close and personal with a bottle of White Out. Now, it's easy to cut and paste, to find a better word choice, to fix a typo, or to catch a grammatical error.

Failure scares us.

We have been conditioned to believe that we can edit and swing multiple times. There is a sense that something is never done. That relationship isn't really over because we're still friends on Facebook. That trip to the Grand Canyon wasn't our only chance to hike, because we can JetBlue out there for a long weekend. That Spiderman movie wasn't the last. There will be sequels and prequels and remakes. Soon. Nothing is ever done or impossible. There is always another chance to do it better the next time.

It's not just that we are used to doing things right, we *value* it. A Career Advisory Board study identified "a sense of accomplishment" as one of Millennials' top three most important factors for career success. Years of conditioning from loving parents has set us up to believe we can do anything we set our minds to. So when we left the nest, we had to encounter something relatively new: failure.

When we were kids, we missed a lot of opportunities to experience rejection or failure naturally. On Valentine's Day, everyone made a paper bag mailbox and got a Valentine from each student in the class. On a classmate's birthday or bar mitzvah, the only reasons you didn't go to their party were because you were out of town or had another party that day. Everyone gets an invitation. Millennials were the first generation to get an A for effort, not for actual success, so even our failures weren't really failures.

Don't get us wrong, we certainly weren't sheltered *entirely* from failure. At least a few times a month we feel like complete and utter losers. An idea will get shot down at work, or we'll drop the ball on a project that doesn't reach its goals, or someone swipes left (Tinder joke, anyone?). We're not immune to coming up short.

We've all experienced rejection and letdowns in our lives. The difference between us and other generations, though, is that expectations have been higher and our missteps cushioned by parents who only want to help. We've experienced failure less (or less severely) than other generations. So now that we're on our own and we have to make some of our own mistakes, you better believe we find that a little scary. So much so that we'll do pretty much anything in our power to avoid it, including pretending it doesn't exist.

We choose, often, to view failure as a starting point, an opportunity to practice for the real deal. It's a video game and we still have a life left. Why? Because most things have typically been up for discussion. We've had teachers we can talk into extra credit and out of detention and parents who were open to negotiating the terms of our grounding because it was a "teaching moment." For us, the word "No" has typically been our jumping-off point.

The point is: we're kind of new at this. The "unlimited lives" policy of our childhood has left us underprepared for failure in the real world. We're not crippled by not knowing failure, but we're certainly still learning how to do it right.

We're eager to try again; we only want to keep learning. XYZ companies give us an environment where we can ask questions and take educated risks. When we get it right, tell us. But tell us when we get it wrong, too. Help us find the value in our mistakes. If you help us learn to recover from our failures, we sure as hell won't quit.

6. WE'RE WIRED

A recent study claimed that older people can juggle maybe five items at once—a cell phone, the TV, a computer on their lap with Twitter and Facebook open. We can juggle more than nine. This means that we can be productive while working on two screens with multiple Gchats and email threads, Facebook open, headphones blasting the new Taylor Swift song in our ears, and iPhone on the desk to monitor the three live iMessage conversations.

Who is more productive? The answer is probably, "it depends." We are certainly better at keeping in contact with multiple people, moving more quickly, researching a new topic, etc. But our point isn't what's better, it's simply to embrace the fact that it's happening. We are simply more than ever. It's a truth.

Your hardware defines you.

If you still carry a Blackberry in a holster on your hip, we're going to judge you. Badly. Worse? If you think it makes sense to pick a machine for us—assign us a phone, assign us a computer, etc.—you are insulting us.

One of the perks we love most is the freedom to select our own equipment. Our devices are expressions of our personality and our most useful appendage. Budget the money and space to allow employees to choose their own machines.

We love laptops. In fact, according to Pew, 70 percent of us prefer a laptop to a desktop. Forcing us to work on a desktop is like chaining many of us to an anchor. Instead, give us a laptop and we might bring our work home, to lunch, and to that meeting in the conference room. We're wired all the time and working on work/personal simultaneously.

7. EVERYTHING WE DO IS PUBLIC

We have zero sense of privacy. We live with strangers we met on Craigslist. We go to coffee with strangers we met through our phones. And we ride in cars with random drivers we find via crowdsourced apps.

So why would you think we should have a line between our work and personal lives? We share our personal life at work and our work life with our personal friends . . . and sometimes we do it all online.

You quietly asked a friend to introduce you to his cute sister or asked a neighbor to make an introduction to his workplace. We post personal ads online and post our entire work history on LinkedIn, including a public note that says we're open to new opportunities.

We talk about everything on social media.

There is no question: your employees are absolutely talking about you and your office on Twitter. So make the most of it. Know that your office inner-workings are now public. Use that to your advantage.

For example, imagine you have twenty employees with an average of 1,000 friends on Facebook. If they each post about your huge weekend sale on flip flops, you've just reach thousands of people . . . for free. Don't block social media at work; make it work for you.

No subject is off limits.

You put a huge sign on your lawn for your favorite candidate or put a bumper sticker on your car that declared your pro-gun views. We'll post our thoughts on Facebook for all to see. And, we might wear a funny T-shirt to work that declares our political leanings.

You might have had a friend set you up with another friend or you'd go on a group date. We post our personal preferences and photos online and go on dates with total strangers.

You were careful to find a doorman building or a close family friend to be your roommate. We post something on Craigslist and move in with a total stranger who responded to our post.

Every subject is fair game, and public.

Shared documents

Printed matter is weird to us. Why use paper? Why make anything so permanent and limited? In fact, we don't even understand why you'd PDF that document. Instead, we live by open calendars, Google Docs, and Trello boards. Work is fluid, shared, and public. It is fundamentally collaborative and live.

IN SUMMARY

The previous seven tenets make up the foundation of *The XYZ Factor*. Read on to find out how DoSometing.org has turned these general learnings into practical applications.

DoSomething's goal is to inspire young people to do more community service. Maybe your company makes lipstick or cars; maybe you work at a recycling plant or drive a school bus. Any company can be an XYZ company. We're here to share our formula with you. This book serves as a window into how we've found success navigating an XYZ world and how any company can do the same. You'll get a sneak peek into best practices on office culture, developing partnerships, building and maintaining brand, measuring data, working with a zero-dollar marketing budget, and more.

Happy reading!
Nancy and Alyssa

ONE

THE PHYSICAL SPACE

• • •

AN OFFICE LIKE SUMMER CAMP

Julie Lorch,
Head of User Experience

T he first thing you have to do if you want to be an XYZ company is create a physical environment where your staff wants to spend their days and weeks. Think about it: we spend more time in the office than in any of the places we are with our families and friends. So please keep that horrid beige cubicle far away!

When guests arrive at the DoSomething.org office, they are confronted with an energetic atmosphere that combines the ethos of a West Coast tech startup with the look and feel of a dazzling, suspenseful comic book.

DoSomething.org's physical environment does its best to maximize play by featuring bright colors and Razor scooters, a Pac-Man arcade game in the kitchen, and superhero-themed conference rooms. Our playful surroundings allow us to deepen our relationships. They inspire our creativity too. All XYZ organizations need an office that is designed to inspire collaboration and flexibility while also allowing enough mental space to get work done well and on time.

Our office's layout grants DoSomething.org employees an all-access pass to each other. We sit in an open floor plan, which gives way to constant collaboration and spontaneous conversations across teams, influencing our decision-making processes and improving our problem-solving skills. Our software choices reinforce this sense of cooperation: the entire office is on a shared calendar and a closed chat. We started by using Google apps, added the likes of HipChat and LucidChart, and now there's nowhere to hide (which is kinda how we like it). No one's behind a closed door and everyone has a vote. It's totally flat, and it's pretty cool.

We're lucky to have a happy and energetic staff, but we're even luckier to have an office environment that's full of fun and surprises while we work. The DoSomething.org office sets the stage for our jobs, of course; but it's also the backdrop for our friendships. Have you ever thought of your office this way?

MAXIMIZE FUN

The first time I walked into DoSomething.org's New York headquarters, I was in awe of the bright cheery space and the groups of excited, friendly young people working on social change projects. Every single person I saw was smiling—in New York. Teams lingered around the airy eighth floor, full of light and happy decorations. I felt like I walked into an interview at a summer camp. Of course my delight was immediately tempered by my distress—how could it be that fun work environments had eluded me until this point in my career? DoSomething was a fun place to be and, as a Gen-Y tech nerd, I wanted to work there immediately.

The DoSomething office is an XYZ office because it doesn't feel like an office at all. It feels like a magical ball pit attached to a jungle gym on the Island of Misfit Toys. It's an environment that celebrates quirky people and their ideas. It's a place to communicate freely and to explore different perspectives. You can let your thirteen-year-old self run free with everyone else's inner child in the ball pit, while the smarts you developed as an old person (at DoSomething, anyone over the age of twenty-six is considered an "old person") hang out on the jungle gym climbing crazy obstacles. And you get to hang out with such awesome people that you almost forget they're technically coworkers.

Tweetable Takeaway
To maximize fun in an XYZ organization, take office cues from summer camp!

The office's offbeat design is specific to DoSomething's US headquarters. The space wasn't designed by architects or a building manager. Instead, a committee of employees from different departments chose

the layout, furniture, and fun surprises—walls painted bright yellow, cartoonish comfy blue sofas sprinkled about, and space bathed in beautiful natural light. Pillars are adorned with puffy yellow- and black-lettered references to office tropes and traditions like Toto Tuesdays, SMS, and Awesome-Sauce. The phrase "Fight for the User," a *Tron* reference, is painted in giant black-and-white lettering on the center wall and in full view of nearly every employee.

Other areas are collaged with notes and images, making the office look a lot like a teenager's bedroom. The Inspiration Wall is a floor-to-ceiling mélange of magazine cutouts and references to celebrities, pop culture, and brands we like. The handiwork of a recent summer intern, the Inspiration Wall includes at least five pictures of Ryan Gosling and happens to hover right next to my current desk (coincidence?).

We also hang birthday cards by our desks. Katie, whose title is Head of Fun, prints an 11 × 17 card for each person on his or her birthday, and coworkers add warm wishes and inside jokes in brightly colored markers. It's like that one page of your yearbook where you had an orange-and-purple marker and everyone was really nice to you. An intern from two summers ago, who's now a full-time employee at DoSomething, turned to me the day before his birthday and said, "If I don't get one of those giant cards, I'm going to be so sad. But don't tell Katie. I want everyone to do it on their own." Of course he got a card. And he promptly displayed it proudly for all to see—a sign demonstrating his membership in our tribe. XYZ organizations mix the personal with the professional. We celebrate birthdays, weddings, babies, and other milestones in fun ways that make individuals feel super special and loved.

There are even a handful of peculiar, playful artifacts in the office that we use to celebrate each other and keep up our fun work culture. If DoSomething were to be excavated in five hundred years, they'd find a Penguin, a gong, an MP3 of Toto's big hit song "Africa," and one mirrored disco ball. These are the XYZ versions of office memos and Employee of the Month plaques. These artifacts shape our identity as a fun, youthful organization—and they help each of us remember that we're part of something far bigger than ourselves.

Tweetable Takeaway

XYZ culture is in the details—fun artifacts around the office complement an airy space.

You're probably thinking—excuse me, a Penguin? Yes, you read it right. The Penguin is a petite but surprisingly heavy stuffed animal whose yellow nose is almost falling off. He wears a Hawaiian lei and a bandana to keep him as adorable and silly as possible, and he's passed

from employee to employee each week in recognition of a special individual achievement at the all-staff meeting every Wednesday. Did Business Development lock a new corporate partner? Did a campaign blow through its goals by 200 percent? These are Penguin-worthy events.

Receiving the Penguin is a big deal. It's a way for a coworker to call attention, in front of the entire office, to something awesome you did. That little guy sits on your desk for a whole week while people congratulate you on your big win. And then you get to watch everyone else do amazing work through the Penguin lens and delightfully choose whom to give it to next. It's the XYZ version of a stale Employee of the Month plaque.

While the Penguin is emblematic of a job well done, the best part of this tradition is that it inspires coworkers to support each other and set one another on a giant, happy pedestal. It doesn't encourage competition or jealousy; rather, it places the focus on respect and celebration. The Penguin is a physical version of a really satisfying high five, where both parties—and everyone nearby—get to hear about how perfectly you slapped hands.

To celebrate a huge DoSomething.org win or to launch a new campaign, we bang a big ol' Wu-Han gong. Loudly. Everyone in the office can hear it, and we all stop what we're doing to gather in The Pit, an area in the center of the office with a cluster of couches dotted with a disco ball (as an aside, put a shiny disco ball in the center of an office and the promise of the next party is subtly omnipresent). Bangs of the gong are met with immediate applause and cheers; they call a community together to celebrate something amazing. We bang it to start parties, to launch campaigns, and to give major announcements. It's a collective ritual that's much better than an office memo, and the loud ringing is far more fun than a loudspeaker or school bell.

Tweetable Takeaway

XYZ organizations celebrate wins—personal milestones and professional achievements demand to be heard!

The gong isn't the only use of sound to signify an event at DoSomething. The office is approximately two hundred times the size of

my tiny apartment in New York, which is the about the same for every employee here. It's a fun place to be: there is always toilet paper (as well as free tampons in the women's restroom), and you're working on cool projects with your friends. It's got all the comforts of home. Who would ever want to leave?

Turns out that's something we actually had to fix. So at 5:30 P.M. every Tuesday, Katie, our Head of Fun, starts playing Toto's "Africa." It begins slowly, a little reminder that you should start to finish up whatever you're working on. But the song is actually on repeat, getting louder and louder until "I bless the rains down in A-a-frica" is blaring so brilliantly that most people in the office just up and leave. The idea behind Toto Tuesday is simple: everyone should have one night when they leave the office at a decent hour and go on a date or do laundry or just watch old *Friends* reruns. Now "Africa" has become our theme song. Wherever we are, if "Africa" comes on, we gather in a huddle and dance.

Every summer camp detail of our office makes us uniquely DoSomething and lets everyone know that we like to have fun at work. I felt it on the first day of my interview, and it's there every single day I come to the office. Of all the reasons why I love my job here, I'm most thankful for the fun.

BE ALL-ACCESS

Two major XYZ values are transparency and democracy. We reflect these values at DoSomething by sitting in an open floor plan and using software that encourages collaboration and allows us to communicate constantly.

And "we" means everyone—from the CEO to the interns, the Tech team, the Campaigns team, Marketing, and Biz Dev. You name it; we're all there, sitting at a giant bay of desks organized into pods of four tables. Each employee has a large, clean workspace and a movable set of unattached drawers. We don't have any offices or cubicles, and the pod layout doesn't include any vertical barriers between employees. Everyone can see everyone else all the time—employees can see colleagues, managers can see teams, teams can see the CEO, and interns can get easily distracted. This lack of vertical clutter is an intentional design choice that's become absolutely critical to our collaborative and transparent culture.

> ### Tweetable Takeaway
> To keep an XYZ organization democratic, get rid of visual barriers in the office!

The lack of vertical barriers gives everyone permission to communicate freely and encourages friendship. Without vertical visual barriers, the organization feels amazingly flat. We are all available to each other, and we understand that the best solutions to our challenges could be sitting in the brains on another team and that a conversation with someone across the office could unearth an innovation we couldn't have conceived of alone. When the entire office is in view, every person becomes your collaborator. We're networked in the most human way possible—by physically working next to each other. We can dip into each other's brains to pull out solutions to our challenges on a whim. I know when I can grab a teammate for an off-the-cuff conversation or help with a problem, because I can actually see when they're free; similarly I know when Nancy, the CEO, is available for quick approval of wireframes or other design ideas. I can immediately find two or three people to stand around a whiteboard for a brainstorm on the fly or gather other random coworkers who look like they might be free too.

The catch is that in addition to your collaborator, everyone now has permission to become your critic. Although an extra pair of eyes can help improve ideas and realize solutions in a more nuanced way, they can also lead to discouragement among teammates.

My view recently included direct access to one of the DoSomething .org designer's screens. It's exciting to see a designer with a big screen full of gorgeous new visual work. It can be a brightly lit invitation for accolades, or a giant sponge to absorb coworkers' millions of tiny tweaks. I could watch each revision over the designer's shoulder, gaining access to an intimate thought process otherwise unavailable to coworkers (yes, I was essentially "eaves-looking"). The designer received constant feedback over the course of two months—eventually leading to distress and even a few tears. No doubt her design would have been very different had she finished most of her work in a cubicle and showed visuals only at key phases of the process; but would it have been stronger or weaker without the constant feedback? Would the process have been more or less stressful for the designer?

Some employees take over empty pillars and walls to host giant timelines and charts or to disseminate information. Dave, the Head of Campaigns, pasted 200 new calls to action on a pillar smack in the middle of the office. His notes became something of a spectacle and catalyst of conversations between those checking out the list, suggesting improvements, and enjoying the lightning strikes of spontaneous collaboration and new ideas. This really indicates Dave's pride in the work his team was producing. It also invites the rest of the staff to comment democratically: that's what DoSomething offers its employees and what XYZers expect.

The open floor plan gives us extra space and freedom to roam.

There is one major lap around DoSomething.org—it goes through the lobby, around the main office, by the gym, through the kitchen, and back to the lobby. We're coming and going around the Lap all the time and we see when people are working individually or brainstorming together. We also see when people are eating lunch, hanging out, or randomly dancing in the middle of the day (the Content team is known for busting out in sporadic dance battles and lip-synchs).

The Lap makes the invitation to collaborate or criticize a completely mobile experience. For example, if a group is hashing out ideas on a whiteboard, it's very easy for someone walking by to add a thought to the mix or a judgment of the work at hand. This person might be on your team, or you may never have had a project with him or her before. At best, work is pushed further. Design solutions and campaign ideas are tightened and improved when an outsider points out that something's missing on the whiteboard. Of course, a mobile critic can prompt the team to unduly jump down rabbit holes or dwell on unnecessary details.

Whether you view this interaction as a benefit or a disruption, I tend to think what really matters is that we always extend the invitation to communicate with each other and consider a new perspective—not only to the other three people in our pods but also to whoever happens to be cruising over to the kitchen. As with any situation, there are pros and cons—and we're constantly working to ensure that the positives outweigh the negatives.

Speaking of cruising, our CTO, Matt, favors a Razor scooter when he's taking a lap. We actually have a few scooters in the office; they're great to use when going from desk to desk, or when people are feeling a little bored and just want to go out for a spin. This means of transportation is fun and energetic, and totally quirky (especially when you see the CTO scoot from desk to desk). But I think the scooters inadvertently cut down on mobile criticism and collaboration, because people are moving too quickly and can't stop to chat. I personally love serendipitous conversations, so I try to walk.

As I remarked in the beginning of the chapter, we've extended this all-access approach to software choices too. We use Google apps for everything. Google Drive is amazing for sharing and collaborating on documents and presentations, and we are always able to access what we need because it lives in the Cloud. In fact, we wrote most of this book using Google Drive. We're also on Gchat to talk throughout the day, which is great for fast answers (and admittedly, to send the occasional cat video). Google Calendar is as all-access as it gets; everyone can see everyone else's calendar to schedule meetings and discover what people are up to at various points in the day. Our COO Aria recounted a story of a time when she was trying to schedule a meeting with someone from another organization and had to go through his assistant. It took forever to schedule because the assistant didn't have access to the calendar!

Aria was baffled; she'd never worked in a place where she wasn't able to see what everyone was doing at every moment of the day.

Tweetable Takeaway
Choose transparent and collaborative software for your XYZ
Company. Google apps are the best!

We also host institutional information with special software to assign an owner, allow for editing, and keep a record of every update. We store product development archives in wikis that we can add to whenever. Everyone in the office is on Trello, a shared project management system where individuals are assigned to specific tasks that they then move from On Deck, to Doing, to Done. The entire office can see the majority of these boards, and oftentimes it's how we like to be informed of requests for work. The Tech and Product teams have a special chat room via HipChat to ask code questions, upload images, and tell jokes, and we use GitHub to host our software development projects. Using GitHub to track code revisions and edit each other's work has become a critical tool for our highly collaborative Tech team. And of course, we use my favorite, LucidChart, a Web-hosting system that allows for collaboration on diagrams, specs, and charts, to develop processes and wireframes together on a shared account.

But when we say all-access, we mean it. At DoSomething, we let our coworkers in on our lives outside of work, and this is one of the most significant components of an XYZ organization. Related to our emphasis on transparency is a specific desire for individual authenticity. We're all connected on Facebook, Twitter, Instagram, Snapchat, and LinkedIn; but XYZers want to be able to show off their individualism in the workplace, too. We bring our tastes, ideas, and moods with us to create a more authentic experience. You can't be bland and boring if you want to be an XYZ organization. Rather, you have to let your employees infuse their personalities into the environment. You have to let them nest.

We post photos, work, cards, and art near our desks. I have a bunch of 3D puzzles and cube bots to play with when I'm stumped.

Our CEO Nancy is the queen of nesting. She adorns her walls with wacky Hello Kitty paraphernalia, including a pair of pink-and-white Hello Kitty roller skates hanging high on a hook above her desk. Some might see the roller skates as a bit ridiculous; but they act as a visual indicator from the CEO herself that it's cool to be yourself here—show us who you are and hang up stuff you like around your space. Those roller skates tell us we're free to be weird and we belong no matter what. This is a gift to XYZers.

Nesting is a big deal for two reasons. First, it indicates our desire to feel personally connected to our workspace. It's a way to take ownership and feel comfortable at the office. XYZers put our individualism on display to coworkers, which gives the office a really personal and familiar feel. It's casual and fun—and that's exactly the kind of environment where I want to spend forty-plus hours per week.

Nesting also encourages authentic communication. Personal artifacts act as a conversation starter. Pictures of Kenia's new baby pasted on her wall, the books about the marriage debate within the LGBT community stacked on Alysha's filing cabinet, and the bottle of whiskey on Crystal's desk are all invitations to break the ice and build a relationship.

Tweetable Takeaway
Personalization and nesting in the office = a happy XYZ community.

DESIGN FOR FRIENDSHIP

We designed the office at DoSomething to inspire friendship. So far we've talked a lot about communication while working, with a dash of unique DoSomething.org details and celebrations. But relationships are maintained and trust is deepened in tiny pockets around the office where people gather when they're not working. These pockets also host spontaneous interactions and side conversations that spark creative solutions. Whether there's comfortable seating, spectacle, or tradition, XYZ organizations must remember to develop the Millennial version of the proverbial water cooler. Think about where people gather in your office—what's your water cooler 2.0?

Let's take, for example, the Coffee Corner in the kitchen. Once upon a time, the Tech team ruled the Corner. This group of geeks (myself included) cared so deeply about the quality of our coffee that we were willing to invest ten to fifteen minutes to prepare a single cup. We would painstakingly measure gram by gram the artisanal beans, lovingly set the grinder to its proper position, boil filtered water to just the right temperature, and choose from a bevy of time-consuming and detail-oriented contraptions from which to brew—the AeroPress, the pourover, the Chemex.

Because the brewing process takes so damn long, we team members were forced to make conversation. It would generally begin with a well-articulated discussion of the current bean selection and the benefits of each brewing methodology. But that would usually just last about two minutes. Someone would eventually have to push the conversation further. How's your day going? What are you working on? The Coffee Corner was the place to befriend your fellow nerds. We even started to bring in beans to share and try.

Tweetable Takeaway

XYZers build relationships around water cooler 2.0 . . . what's yours?

Obviously, once non-nerds tasted the superiority of our coffee, they wanted to learn how to brew properly. I relished this turn of events and took time to teach coworkers the joy of the pourover. A surprisingly large number of people mentioned that they'd wanted to know how to use the AeroPress for months, but found the steps too intimidating. Non-nerds started to mix with the Tech team in the Coffee Corner, and we all started conversations with each other relating to our favorite beans.

Then, we made conversation as we waited. Last summer I hashed out a design solution to our global navigation problem with a Content intern. Maxwell, a favorite front-end developer, shared his anxieties about leaving DoSomething after receiving an amazing job offer. I taught Darren from Biz Dev how to make a pourover, and we talked about new angles of pitching product development to partners.

I can claim without a shadow of a doubt that the conversations in the Coffee Corner are superior (and far longer!) to those around the lobby water cooler, where all you have to do is push a button and hold a cup under the tap.

The Coffee Corner sits to the side of the kitchen, which extends to a large lunchroom with long picnic tables and about thirty chairs—another

informal gathering spot where friendships take root. The walls are decorated with hundreds of framed awards and news articles about DoSomething.org. We're not allowed to eat at our desks—a policy that's technically due to the tiny mouse problem we have in the office, but one that's spawned a ridiculously fun lunch hour. We can take our lunch whenever the mood strikes, walk on over to the kitchen, and hang out and eat with whoever is there. The long tables ensure that we sit together and talk to each other. Employees also come in early to eat breakfast with whoever's around; they head to the kitchen for a snack in the afternoon or a quick round of Pac-Man—and sometimes even eat dinner together if they're staying late.

The most amazing thing about these meals together is that these XYZers never talk about work. After a year at DoSomething.org, I can count on one hand the number of times I've been asked a work-related question at lunch—most of which were accompanied by a pre-question apology. You know that you're going to get a break from shoptalk when you sit down at the table. Lunch is a time to tell jokes, tease each other about dumb things, and talk about our personal lives. Regardless of which team they're on or whatever their stress level is that day, lunch is where people get to know each other.

Lunch breaks have had another significant benefit: the big tables and the kitchen's overall design (which includes other gathering spots such as the microwave, staff fridge, sink, and dishwasher) coupled with the fact that we're not allowed to eat at our desks, have rendered in-office cliques nearly obsolete.

Tweetable Takeaway

XYZers love to hang. What would happen if everyone in your office still took a lunch hour?

Nearby sits another nonworking space, the Gym. It's tiny, maybe 15 × 15 square feet, small enough to house a few machines and smell your grody coworkers. But, like the Coffee Corner, the Gym gives rise to some unanticipated bonds that are unrelated to work. For example, one of the data guys, Josh, was training for a marathon last year. He used the Gym quite a bit, around the same time Keri, a cardio enthusiast from the Design team, was working out. Bryce, a new member of the Content team—and male model—would also hop in after work. Josh, Keri, and Bryce almost never, ever work together on projects, but working out together helped them to get to know each other.

A final space that blends working and hanging out sits off to the side in a corner of the main office. The Ha-Ha-Hacienda is like a living room designed by a wide-eyed eight-year-old. Yes, it's a reference to the Joker's lair, where the evil villain laughed maniacally as he crafted plans to try to thwart Batman. We certainly aren't in the evildoing business, but we do use the lair to chill out and think up new stuff. The Hacienda takes up a corner off to the side of the office and is packed with comfortable sofas under a dozen blue-and-green paper lanterns. There is a whiteboard there too, perpetually full of scribbles of ideas and planning. Sometimes we hold meetings in the Hacienda; sometimes we work with our laptops resting on cushy pillows; and every now and then, you can catch someone taking a power nap (an activity recently OK'd and personally sampled by management). There are also stacks of games, from Taboo to Settlers of Catan. Pretty much everyone on staff wanders into the Hacienda from time to time. The space provides the perfect space to unwind during the day.

The time we spend together not working—either around the Coffee Corner, at lunch, in the Gym, in the Hacienda, or elsewhere around the

office—gives us the opportunity to become friends in addition to being coworkers. After all, the average person spends more time with their coworkers than with their families or friends. So, we ought to like each other, know each other, and support each other.

The environment itself—the office design, the open space, and the playful atmosphere—lets us have fun while we work, lets us be people not just workers, and encourages us to collaborate. There aren't cliques or secret meetings. Of course, this isn't appropriate for every line of work; but if individual companies challenged themselves to create their own vision of summer camp—a physical space where employees feel connected to each other and are encouraged to enjoy their work—a lot of people would be a lot happier at work. And happier employees are more productive and engaged employees.

SWAP SEATS

There is a need in an open floor plan for designated areas to support different modes of work. When DoSomething.org employees feel stuck, we can pick up and move to about a dozen different spots in the office. It offers us a sense of freedom throughout the day, and a variety of postures—everything from standing desks to sofas. Our office changes from hour to hour and evolves over time; not only do we swap desks twice a year in a tradition known as the Reaping, but we also decorate the office and throw a massive party every other month. The space is adaptable—and so is the team.

Tired of sitting? Grab a standing desk by the window. Want to soften the blow of a crushing workload? Veg out on one of the cushy blue sofas around the office. Need to chat with a teammate about a quick issue? Roll on over to their desk and hash it out. Since we all use laptops and have abundant Wi-Fi throughout the office, we can work in virtually every nook and cranny.

Moving around and seat swapping even lends itself to employees feeling comfortable playing different roles. I've never heard a DoSomething staff member say, "That's not my job," or "Not my problem"—ever. XYZers want to be flexible, and we want options. Successful XYZ organizations expertly harness this restlessness.

But here is one major problem with an open floor plan: it can be awkward attempting to talk on the phone or hold a small meeting without the entire office hearing every last word (even though only a few of us actually have phones on our desks). So we did make some barriers. There are two small phone booths, sound-proofed and outfitted with a DoSomething.org background for video conferences calls. A phone booth is a must for offices embracing open floor plans!

There are also six conference rooms for group work and small meetings, each of varying size, each possessing superpowers. When you look up available rooms to book in our shared Google Calendar, you'll find names of superhero lairs like 20 Ingram Street, where Peter Parker lived with his Aunt May. This small conference room has a giant web made of black yarn on the wall and rubber spiders hanging all over the place. Most of the conference rooms are decked out with whiteboards and big screens to hook up computers and share work. But none of these spaces feels like a standard conference room. Even though serious work happens here, they have playful details like an imposing red chandelier in Themyscira and plastic toy bats hanging in the Batcave.

DoSomething staff is like liquid, flowing through the office all day long. Each employee grows into the full space, rather than just their desk. We also develop tendencies: Maxwell, on the Tech team, often uses a standing desk. Crystal, from the Data team, sits in a small room with her full spectrum light on during the winter. Mike, on Product, usually snacks and works in the lunchroom around 3 P.M. I always book

Themyscira, because I find the lighting from the red chandelier to be calming. We are allowed—indeed, encouraged—to develop work habits in spaces that suit us. And as a result, we often feel ownership over these spaces. Employees connected to a space where they do their best work want to come to work every day.

Tweetable Takeaway
Engineer serendipity to keep XYZers on their toes!

We make sure everyone shakes loose from time to time too. We've come to engage in a ritual we call the Reaping, a seating lottery we host about twice a year (it's a heavy title for what is actually a happy tradition). At 9 A.M. on the day of the Reaping, everyone drops their name into a hat to be picked out one by one. When your name is picked, you have fifteen seconds to choose a new desk. This tradition works because we are totally mobile to begin with. After the lottery, we grab our laptops, desk toys, and rolling filing cabinets and head over to our new workspace. The Reaping induces panic and stress. We count down the days until the morning. We strategize, consider top picks, and discuss options with teammates (there was discussion of a secondary market, but that has yet to happen). Everything happens by chance; we have no idea where we'll be sitting—or whom we'll be next to—by the end of the day. The very act of the Reaping reinforces the collective emphasis on individual flexibility. Mental flexibility follows environmental and physical flexibility—I challenge your XYZ organization to a Reaping.

The day of the Reaping is big event, and every single seat is up for grabs. People arrive extremely early, because if you miss your turn your name goes back into the hat for later—and that is basically the most gut-wrenching feeling ever, like having to miss your own birthday party because you're stuck at home with the flu. Some teams cluster in certain areas; the Tech team favors the quieter "dark side," away from the sunny windows facing 21st Street, while the Marketing team, Biz Dev, and Campaigns team prefer to line the windows along the "light side." As the pods slowly fill up with new neighbors, those yet to be picked re-strategize over the remaining open desks. The last people chosen grab a desk from whatever's left, with about as much control over who their new neighbors are as the few people whose names were chosen first and selected desks in empty pods.

The Reaping is a great opportunity to press restart. Staff members clear out papers and clutter, polish old desks, and arrive at a sparkling clean, brand-new workspace by 10 A.M. A clear, spacious desk gives us a clear, spacious brain.

The creative energy that comes with a new spot, a fresh start, and the promise of time and conversation with new neighbors is exciting. Reapings have pulverized any cliques, as the new seating mixes up talent, teams, and cliques. Each Reaping feels like the start of a new job from a different perspective, which keeps the office energized—and restless Millennials on their toes.

There's one other way to keep Millennials employed, and that is to throw a ton of awesome parties. XYZers have really blurred lines when it comes to mixing work and fun. Our office supports our work, but it is flexible enough that it also supports our parties too. Have you ever thrown a Christmas party in your office that turned into an outrageous dance battle? How many times last year did you decorate your workspace with streamers and balloons?

That the staff is happy and relaxed enough to party in the office speaks volumes about the vitality of our team. We don't have to "get out of the office" to have fun. We move the desks around to set up kegs and a DJ booth, and we invite all our friends from outside of the office to come hang out too. In short—keep the space flexible, throw a bunch of parties, and swap seats, and you'll keep your XYZers happy.

REMEMBER THE INTROVERTS

Our all-access office environment and culture of celebration suits extroverts—those who are energized by social connections with coworkers. But not everyone on our team is an extrovert; in fact, certain types of work lure introverts to DoSomething.org (i.e., the people who write code all day long to power our website). So how do introverts cope with the lack of physical barriers and the flood of communication all day? And how might this work for the introverts in your company?

The short answer: it's a challenge. I'm not a shy person, but I am absolutely introverted. When I first started at DoSomething.org, I was completely cashed out every Friday afternoon. And it wasn't because of how hard I was working. I was just tired of communicating for eight hours a day.

If we introverts wish to thrive in a physical environment that favors extroverts, we have to develop some sneaky work-arounds. For example—during the last Reaping, I immediately changed to the only desk in the entire office that faces a wall. People still walk by on their way to a conference room and of course come over to talk about work and hang out; but I don't stare directly at any other coworkers and I don't have a view of all the action. There is a swivel chair in play that makes it really easy to take a peek at the action or quickly see what's up with someone I need, but then I just swivel right back around and focus on my work.

I also started to block off one or two hours a day on my calendar to get in the zone—time in which I was not allowed to chat, collaborate, or attend a meeting. As a product manager, sometimes I need to stick my face in flowcharts and wireframes for hours to develop strategy and documents to work from. And as an introvert, sometimes I need to stop talking. The phrase "Heads Down" pops up in short blocks all over my calendar—and since everyone in the organization uses Google apps, everyone can see it. My awesome coworkers respect my Heads Down time, whether or not they know it's there for me to recharge.

Meanwhile, the open office floor plan has given rise to a sacrosanct Headphone Culture at DoSomething.org that's revered by introverts and extroverts alike. In addition to laptops, new hires are outfitted with giant noise-blocking headphones that match everyone else's. Because we don't have any barriers between our desks, let alone a door to an office, head-phones act as a visual cue for employees to know whether their colleague is concentrating on a task (or not!). We share tons of music throughout the day, creating a sea of head bobbers and foot tappers. Some people put the music on mute and simply wear headphones so as not to be disturbed (April, the head of DoSomething.org's International expansion, is a regular silent headphone wearer).

Regardless of whether a DoSomething.org employee is introverted or extroverted, everyone needs time to focus during the day. Strong code demands concentration; good design takes time; smart content requires a ton of attention to detail; and sometimes headphones just aren't enough. You may be wondering how—in the midst of our laps around the office, lack of physical barriers, and gong banging—anyone gets any work done?

I'm pretty sure our CTO, Matt, started asking that very same question a few months after he started last year. One idea that's caught on is "Thinking Thursdays," where everyone in the office agrees to be silent for a three-hour block of time on Thursday afternoon. Zero meetings are scheduled, no chatting is allowed, and almost everyone is hooked up to headphones. The office-wide study hall is utterly painful for some of the more extroverted staff. But just as we push introverts in this dynamic space, we do the same for extroverts during Thinking Thursdays.

Matt also came up with the idea of Sprints, a one-day work-from-anywhere option when employees can knock out a solid eight-hour chunk of work. Initially, this idea was totally counter to the DoSomething.org way of life—being together, being collaborative, being in that open floor space is who we are. But Matt identified a need that our open office plan warranted and Sprints began on a tenuous trial basis.

Each employee was granted one Sprint day per quarter. As we started to take advantage of these solid work hours—still plugged in to chat and e-mail throughout the day in case anyone needed us—our productivity improved and huge deliverables started coming in ahead of time. Before we knew it, we were given one Sprint a month.

> **Tweetable Takeaway**
> Remember the introverts in an XYZ company—their engines require different fuel.

IN SUMMARY

XYZ organizations create a place where work happens but where play is just as important. They maximize fun, allow people unlimited access to each other, are designed to build friendships, and even let us swap seats (just remember to keep the introverts happy too!). If DoSomething was a summer camp, we'd have an awesome lineup of sports and arts and crafts in the morning for fun, canteen time for bunks to hang out with each other, challenging low ropes courses to build friendships, and musical chair tournaments again and again. Then, a few of us would sleep every rest hour after lunch.

What can you do to make your office feel more like a summer camp? The first step is to think about play more than work.

QUESTIONS TO GET YOU STARTED

1. What three words would you use to describe your physical office layout?

2. Does your office design favor introverts or extroverts?

3. Where are the spaces in your office where employees are able to build personal relationships with each other?

4. How could your work environment support more serendipitous conversations?

5. Does your office environment encourage fun?

6. How does your office determine where people sit, when they move, and who gets a window? Is it based on seniority or on fostering collaboration and creativity?

7. When is a closed door necessary?

8. How does your company celebrate big wins and individual achievements?

9. Does your office have a theme song or something else that unites everyone?

10. Are light and color used purposefully in your office?

11. Would you want to work in an XYZ office?

ABOUT THE CONTRIBUTOR

Julie is Head of User Experience at DoSomething.org. She spends most of her day making wireframes for software products that support young people making an impact on their communities. She loves bikes and flowcharts and considers herself a friendly introvert. She also brews a mean pourover.

TWO

PITCH, PLEEEEASE

• • •

HOW XYZ ORGANIZATIONS MAKE PRESENTING A WAY OF LIFE

Julie Lorch,
Head of User Experience

Everyone at DoSomething.org knows that that the best ideas can come from anyone in the room; this is a key XYZ value. It's a belief that's both empowering and democratic, and it's the backbone of our entrepreneurial office environment. But there are a lot of smart people in the room, all with great ideas. So if you think you have the best idea, it's up to you to get it out there. You have to pitch it.

Pitching is a way of life at DoSomething. We're always doing it, because we're all invested in the future of our organization and looking for ways to improve who we are and what we do. So we pitch each other, we pitch the whole office, we pitch our bosses, and our bosses pitch us too. We pitch in big open forums and in tiny brainstorms on a whiteboard. We're encouraged to challenge the status quo, and we take hundreds of little chances a day and thousands a year doing so. But here's the really important thing: pitching at DoSomething.org isn't really about ego. It's about vulnerability. And over time, it's allowed us to develop an authentic, earnest culture of pitching.

It's also is a form of risk taking; remember, we never know whose idea will be the best in the room. Pitches are generally met with collaboration, questions, and debate—rarely with unanimous praise and approval. So when we pitch, we are also learning how to react to criticism. We learn that some of our ideas suck. And we learn to take responsibility for failure. But most important, we learn to be vulnerable in front of each other.

It's hard, of course; but it's also awesome. I've never been in a work environment where pitching is so radical, or where exposing yourself and your ideas is so much a part of everyday life. And as a result, the employees in this office trust each other deeply. When it comes to innovating and relationship building, pitching rocks.

We have a series of weekly, quarterly, and yearly events to keep pitching alive and well at DoSomething.org. Some events support innovation; some celebrate success; and still others focus on failure. But all allow us the opportunity to pitch, take risks, and experience vulnerability and trust. Let's take a look at some of the hits.

> **Tweetable Takeaway**
> Get up and pitch your idea. XYZ organizations praise individual initiative.

PITCHING NEW IDEAS

The best way to succeed at DoSomething is to have a great idea and run with it. XYZers respond to this high level of autonomy and creativity—and even though sometimes it can be totally intimidating, it works. If you can create a space where anyone can pitch and see their idea through to execution, you stimulate the inception of more and more ideas. It's an amazing feeling for individuals on staff, and it makes the wins even more celebratory.

Every Wednesday morning is our Innovation Meeting. We pitch each other big ideas by saying, "Let's DoSomething.org about: _____." Wednesdays include goals, data, strategies, or pivots, but they are always new and always smart. It's called an "innovation meeting" for a reason, and it's sacred.

People from every team load into one of the large conference rooms and become active members of the presentation. Our COO, Aria, maintains the calendar and sends out e-mails ahead of time with reminders: "Tomorrow, Alysha will present on SMS churn strategy!" or "Don't miss Jeff's presentation on member data!" Alysha and Jeff work out all the kinks of their presentations ahead of time, and even show their pitches to four or five other coworkers to get their input.

Innovation meetings are positive and fun, but they are also an open forum for debate and collaboration. For example, the Tech team might give a presentation about the new Style Guide (a brand book that dictates visual design), and the Campaigns team is able to ask clarifying questions or offer suggestions for improvement. Any big initiative has to go through an innovation meeting, which builds consensus and achieves transparency across the organization. It's also great for knowledge sharing; Wednesday mornings are chock-full of teachable moments.

The pitches themselves generally involve a PowerPoint, some data, a lot of jokes, and a series of next steps. Presenters practice ahead of time and refine their ideas. They try to predict potential criticism and how certain individuals will react, and come up with explanations ahead of time. By the time Wednesday morning rolls around, presenters are really well prepared—and they have to be. Not only is most of the office going to show up; so is your manager, everyone else's manager, and probably Nancy and Aria too. It's a crash course in public speaking and vulnerability.

Everyone is a little nervous before their presentations, and not all pitches are well received. Some instigate questions that the presenter hasn't considered, which can open space for collaboration—or knock your pitch right on its ass. You've got to be good on your toes if you don't know the answer, and chances are, there's something you won't know the answer to. But one thing's for sure—innovation meetings are never boring. A mind-numbing presentation at an innovation meeting will almost certainly be the kiss of death for your idea.

But some topics are boring by nature, right—necessary evils for an organization to discuss? Well, no, not in an XYZ organization. The first innovation meeting I gave was about flowcharts, the most horridly boring subject matter of all time. But I really wanted DoSomething.org to begin structuring workflows in a more logical manner; as we were growing in size it became critical to silo roles and document dependencies with increasingly complex matrix teams. You're probably already bored after reading that sentence!

But it was simple: in order to ship products faster, we had to adopt flowcharts. My presentation involved bright colors and a day in the life of a Chipotle customer—a role every DoSomething.org employee can identify with. A few pretty hilarious flowcharts later, mostly revolving around whether or not to fork over an extra $1.50 for guacamole, I had my audience hooked—because I pitched flowcharts using a relatable, funny example; pulled people on board; and offered to teach anyone who was interested. Now, thanks to that extra scoop of guac, there are flowcharts all over the place at DoSomething.org.

Any employee at DoSomething.org can pitch a solution or take a problem and run with it. The Innovation Meeting tradition provides a fertile, flexible environment that maintains the organization's ability to pivot, and it is the very foundation of our pitch culture here at DoSomething.org.

Tweetable Takeaway

XYZ pitches have to be fun and entertaining to be successful—boring ideas die much faster!

Creative Lunches

Pitches related to art and design have their own convention that we developed during our most recent website redesign. Because we wanted the entire organization to feel a sense of ownership of our new brand, visual design, and content, Nancy decided to open up the design process to anyone interested in a series of weekly Creative Lunches.

Everything would make a debut at these lunches—concepts for new PSAs, business card mock-ups, home page user experience, new boilerplate language, and so on. This represented a huge shift for us—historically, the people on our creative team rarely pitched ideas to the full office. They had operated in a creative silo and revealed only the most beautiful and polished work to much fanfare. This also meant that the majority of designers on staff weren't accustomed to the sense of vulnerability that many of their coworkers experienced every day. Designers didn't trust non-designers with creative decisions.

At first, Creative Lunches were pretty much a total nightmare. Designers hated them; they categorically did not want to pitch concepts, which were often sketches and not as translatable to non-designers as a fully articulated vision. They feared the dreaded design-by-committee trend that suffocates creative innovation. There was also a bit of a language barrier, because coherent design criticism requires a specialized vocabulary. In the midst of a frenetic redesign, teaching non-designers the definition of kerning felt like a time sink.

A lot of this early frustration owes to a pitch scenario that wasn't as democratic as the office was accustomed to. The language barrier and some employees' specialized skills meant that the best ideas were coming exclusively from these individuals. If we wanted to make the creative process more transparent, then we'd have to pry it open with a crowbar.

We had to improve the pitch environment at Creative Lunches—and we began by working on our language skills. Designers took the time to explain terms like "kerning," and product people discussed tap size and the reach of teen thumbs. Marketing explained why we couldn't use the word "suck" with certain partners. While we were technically talking through new creative projects, we spent most of our time learning about all of the details. After a lot of long Creative Lunches, Biz Dev now knows what "visual hierarchy" means. The Campaigns team agrees that we need one major call to action on each page, and they can explain how two buttons instead of one would change conversion rates. It slowed the process to a painful degree, but because of the incredible amount of knowledge sharing, we are a more powerful team.

Tweetable Takeaway

Design for all—find a way to help the whole XYZ office feel like a part of brand decisions.

The second thing we did, at Nancy's insistence, was to eliminate the phrase "I like . . ." No longer were people allowed to say such things as "I like that page" or "I don't like version B." Nancy called you out if you started a sentence with this phrase; you'd have to immediately reword your comment to focus on the reasoning: "This page is stronger because the title is more readable than the other options, and I agree that the call to action should be placed above the fold." More information, right? Eliminating "I like" from Creative Lunches was the single most effective means for the organization to quickly develop a design vocabulary. And the designers responded far better, because they were able to more clearly understand their peers.

Creative Lunches stopped being so frustrating and started becoming a democratic experience. Designers pitched ideas, received a round of feedback, and improved their work. Prying open the creative process offered designers the chance to be vulnerable in front of their peers. It broke down the divide between designers and non-designers, and instilled a sense of trust between them. The quality of the work improved.

With a slew of vocabulary lessons and a fierce commitment to building a culture of design, Creative Lunches eventually leveled the playing field. It took some time, but now the best creative ideas can come from anyone in the room.

LEARN BY EXAMPLE

DoSomething's State of the Union dinners are just one way for us to watch Nancy and Aria in action. Nancy is the queen of pitches, completely mesmerizing in front of a crowd—and even more persuasive one-on-one. We all learn from watching her. She writes LinkedIn columns full of chutzpah and runs our Twitter feed with one bold opinion after another. Every time Nancy pitches DoSomething.org to the world, more and more people fall in love with her.

That's because she pitches with authenticity, humor, and a bit of vulnerability. She admits to staff when she's made an error, and she jumps into action during PR Crisis Management. She's an entrepreneur at heart and wants us all to feel like we can start whatever we want.

Aria, DoSomething.org's COO and Number Two, can captivate a crowd at the drop of a hat. She ran the show at our twentieth anniversary dinner, hosting more than six hundred people and raising over a million dollars that night alone. She's energetic and confident, and she is the master of long intentional pauses.

Aria and Nancy also present at the innovation meeting. They get up with everyone else and share their own one-minute accomplishments, goals, and requests. They're at Fail Fest, Success Fest, Creative Lunches, and job interviews. They aren't "higher ups"—they're a part of the team. XYZ organizations are flat, and these two are right there with us taking risks and making mistakes. We learn by example. What would it be like if your C-suite behaved this way?

The employees at DoSomething may have been hired with some capacity to pitch, but we got so damn good at it by imitating Nancy and Aria.

Tweetable Takeaway

XYZ C-suites are never in the suite—they're pitching, risk taking, and mistake making just like the rest of us.

PITCHING YOURSELF

While we pitch ideas at DoSomething, we also pitch ourselves. Yes, we're very collaborative—we work on teams, we ask for opinions, we are constantly communicating. But wins are often individual, and we don't underestimate the role of social capital. From the moment we interview and then every day after, we show up to play and work and be awesome. Give XYZers the stage, the microphone, or the soapbox and they'll step up into the limelight and embrace their time to shine (as long as everyone can get to the stage and it's really supportive and sometimes full of applause).

Accomplishments, Goals, Requests

We have a lot of meetings on Wednesdays. The All-Staff Meeting, which takes place on Wednesday afternoons at 3:30 P.M., is mandatory. We have a staff of about fifty, and each person has one minute to stand up and give a summary of something amazing they accomplished last week, an important goal they have for next week, and any requests they might have of coworkers. We think of this tradition as a one-minute pitch of yourself and your work every week.

No matter how stressed we are or how many deadlines are looming, we are never allowed to skip a staff meeting. It's an essential tradition for a variety of reasons. First, we come together as a whole and give our collective attention to one another for an hour. When was the last time you stood up in front of your entire office and explained an accomplishment you were proud of? These mini pitches are a time to focus on celebrations. They allow—some might even say force—individuals, regardless of how extroverted or introverted they might be, to brag a little about the things they've done.

Members of the Campaigns team cite numbers of signups and new members in current campaigns; members of Marketing describe recent articles and media impressions; Biz Dev can announce a new partnership; and Tech describes a new module they created. In addition to allowing each other some time to shine, our staff meeting also helps us to understand what everyone works on all day. It lets us see how we're progressing toward shared and individual goals.

The staff meeting builds momentum and excitement around projects. For example, Nami, a member of the Campaigns team, launched a campaign that asked our members to send birthday cards to young people experiencing homelessness living in shelters. It was one of the biggest successes of the year, and every week she'd update the team on another goal the campaign passed.

It's also a great opportunity to give props and pitch someone else's work. At least two or three times a meeting, someone recognizes a teammate for absolutely crushing their goals. It's a huge morale boost when someone notices how well you're doing and celebrates it on your behalf. We take pride in our work, we celebrate our wins, and we cheer for each other—for one hour, every week.

But the Staff Meeting isn't just about success. A whole range of emotions come out during these one-minute pitches. I've heard people express significant frustration with certain projects, and I've heard staff-wide apologies for being a jerk. I've seen people express heartfelt appreciation for working here. I've seen tears in presenters' eyes and tears in everyone listening. The staff meeting is also a forum to ask for help, especially if you're working on a specifically difficult goal for the next week, or if you've been hunting someone down for a meeting for days.

Employees know that the staff meeting is a safe space—a place where people feel comfortable discussing personal battles or achievements. One staff member is battling stage four melanoma, and every so often she uses her time during staff meetings to make a brief announcement about her treatment. She knows how much the team cares about her, and we all want to know how to help. Another staff member, Mike, donated bone marrow after discovering he was a match in the Bone Marrow Registry (which, by the way, he signed up for during our cheek swabbing for Give A Spit campaign). At a recent staff meeting, he read a letter of thanks from the boy who received his donation. We learned about the fact that Mike saved a life at a Staff Meeting. I can't think of a better way to spend an hour.

> **Tweetable Takeaway**
> Create some space for individuals to shine in collaborative XYZ offices.

Staff Meetings are designed to keep the organization transparent by highlighting accountability and celebrating wins, but they also blur the lines of personal and professional subject matter. It might be due to the fact that the staff skews young, and we're able to be so candid with each other. Maybe it's because we have a management team that leads by example, standing up to describe their goals and accomplishments along with everyone. But again, we trust each other enough to be open and vulnerable at work. It's authentic and earnest.

Tweetable Takeaway
Build an XYZ culture of transparency + accountability with weekly stand-up meetings.

Want a Job at DoSomething.org? Pitch, Pleeeease

A huge part of the hiring process at DoSomething.org is evaluating how candidates pitch. If they can do so confidently and with a sense of humor, they'll be comfortable in our energetic environment and fit in with the culture of risk taking.

After a standard phone interview or two and a brief meeting with a staff member, potential employees are cordially invited to the office for an afternoon in the hot seat. When I was invited back to "meet a few more people on the team," I had no idea that I'd sit in the same room for three hours while rotating pairs of current employees sat down for fifteen minutes apiece to grill me. I didn't realize it at the time, but I had to pitch myself, my skills, and my desire to work at DoSomething .org over and over again. It was completely exhausting but also totally rewarding—it reinforced my desire to work here because I understood the level of camaraderie, rigor, and challenges that would await me.

During this three-hour interview, potential employees are also asked to bring in some homework that involves coming up with a new concept or a challenge to the status quo. My assignment when interviewing for product manager was to explain how I'd improve DoSomething's home page. There were about a million things wrong with the home page at the time—but I distilled the top five issues to palatable suggestions. I tried to think of a strategy for explaining to my potential boss and others on the Product and Tech teams how what they'd been doing was completely wrong. By doing so, I got the job.

Employees are invested in the future of the organization. We are always excited about improving who we are and how we do things, and we want to talk about ideas that will push us forward. Potential employees have to reveal small seeds of this powerful sentiment, too.

It's especially important that candidates know how to pitch, because new hires are expected to hit a home run in the first three months of work: that is, achieve a big, measurable win that individuals own and feel proud of. For example: Biz Dev should plan to lock a new partner, Product should expect to increase specific conversions by 10–15 percent, and Campaigns should exceed membership goals by, like, a billion.

We hire people who we believe will thrive when exposed to DoSomething's entrepreneurial spirit. Though we are incredibly collaborative and supportive, we emphasize the role of the individual in innovation and pushing things forward.

This is why we have a role at DoSomething.org called the QB (yes, for Quarterback). The QB is the key person who's heading up an initiative or a project, whose job it is to blend vision, strategy, and project management. The QB pitches an idea and gets it done, with the expectation that he or she will learn the necessary skills to make it happen. This is the most exciting part; we're able to teach each other skills, share knowledge, and constantly learn new things.

Of course, this is a lot of pressure for potential and future employees—one friend and I liken working at DoSomething.org to being a dolphin at SeaWorld. Most of the time you stay underwater, swimming around out of sight. But every now and then, you have to jump up out of the water, do a trick and a backflip with a giant splash, and receive mega applause from everyone watching. Then, you have to get right back in the water. In other words, prepare for a big win, announce the win at staff meeting—then get your head back to prepping your next win.

Tweetable Takeaway

XYZ organizations are collaborative, but individual wins push innovation and help us take pride in our work.

PITCHING FAILURE

Of course, it would be impossible to have so many wins and celebrations without experiencing some failures too. As with other pitches, individuals take responsibility for shortcomings, poor choices, and the occasional horrible disaster. Part of being an XYZ organization is embracing failure and supporting those who fell short so we can all learn from mistakes. If your organization adopts only a single pitch tradition, adopt the Fail Fest (pink boa optional).

Fail Fest

You know what else you have to pitch at DoSomething.org? Your total, abject failures. You have to do it in a pretty similar fashion to pitching your successes—confidently, humorously, and genuinely. And you have to do it while wearing a pink boa.

We call it Fail Fest—not Fail Hell or Fail Guilt—because that's how we approach failure at DoSomething.org: it's OK and it happens to everyone, but you have to own it alongside everyone else. This means learning about why and how you failed and then teaching everyone else about your downward spiral in a public forum so other members of your team are less likely to take that same path.

How did you react the last time you failed at work? Were you afraid you'd be fired? Did you take ownership of it or blame it on someone else? How an organization reacts to failure does more to shape communication and leadership than the way it reacts to success.

Fail Fest takes place once a year. It's a time to say, "I've totally screwed up a strategy, task, or goal sometime this year. Pretty much everyone knows that something I pitched earlier, or something I was confident that I could handle, turned into a mess that affected other people." People can volunteer to present at Fail Fest, or a manager can suggest that someone present—knowing that this individual is at the top of the list of this year's magnificent failures. Presenters talk about what they wanted to do, what went wrong, what was learned personally, and what DoSomething.org learned overall—and then they pitch a comeback.

The most defining characteristic of Fail Fest is that only individuals can present; we're not allowed to share a collaborative fail. In Nancy's words, "The entire point is for one person to take responsibility, discuss what he/she has learned individually, and feel vulnerable in front of a crowd. It's not something to be shared and balanced." Besides, there's only one pink boa.

Last Fail Fest, Baylee of the Biz Dev team stood up and explained how and why they hadn't locked enough partnerships this year. Our cash flow was tight, and members of the management team had to go into emergency fundraising mode. The issue was the timeline of their funnel; the team hadn't done enough in January to be solvent in August. They proposed two changes: The first was to sign corporate partners eight to ten months ahead of time. The second was to create sector silos. Baylee became in charge of Cosmetics and Candy, Darren was on Sports Apparel and Insurance, and Muneer became the Auto and Salty Snacks guy. Baylee took full responsibility. The team was able to put the stress and anxiety of the failure behind them and pivot toward a new goal.

By celebrating failures, we institutionalize the knowledge learned from the experience and develop a culture of responsiveness. We make it OK to say, "I failed this time, but I can—and will—do it better next time." It pushes people to continue to take risks and innovate. Especially in the tech space, we have to acknowledge shortcomings and failure in order to iterate and improve. But this type of rapid development is a great lesson for individuals throughout the organization—in Biz Dev, Campaigns, Content, and everyone else.

Tweetable Takeaway

Be XYZ—celebrate failures and develop a culture of responsiveness.

Pitching failure makes your successes sweeter, but it also keeps you grounded. We support each other in our failures and successes. Fail Fest keeps us adaptable and shapes us into stronger leaders.

State of the Union Dinner + Fishbowl

There's even an opportunity for Nancy and Aria to pitch the team. When we're interviewing a job candidate, one thing we're asked to assess is, "Would I want to be in a bunker with this person?" In other words, would this person have our back in the most dire of circumstances? It's also important that we know our bosses have our backs. And part of that is being open about decision-making processes, but they also have to fulfill unmet needs and, in this particular office, they have to be authentic.

Although the office makes every effort to be as transparent as possible, there's always room for improvement. As our team grew, questions about policies and organizational priorities started cropping up. We weren't sure when or why we were doing certain things—and in an organization that finds strength in democracy, this was an issue that had quietly started to brew.

Nancy, who was not about to allow any middle school gossip to enter our environment, hit the problem head-on. She announced a new tradition: quarterly State of the Union dinners. Yes, we get together and eat and talk about the future. But what's crazy and unique is the way we do it. We use a fishbowl.

I'm not talking about the participatory conversation found in Open Space Technology conferences. I mean the way high schoolers ask embarrassing questions in Sex Ed: by dropping an anonymous question into a fishbowl for the Phys Ed teacher to answer in front of the class. You can ask whatever you want, about any topic at DoSomething.org, and Nancy and Aria will give you a genuine answer—in front of everyone. And they don't open the fishbowl until a few minutes before the State of the Union.

The first dinner included questions like, "What is the path to management here?" and "What if our pivot to restructuring the member experience to focus on campaigns FAILS?" Some other gems were: "What's your favorite and least favorite part about your role?" and "How much cash do we have on hand? What's our monthly burn?" Nancy and Aria talked through each of these questions and many others, pitching us answers, being a little more vulnerable than usual in front of the group, and gaining a pretty clear understanding of where the team's anxieties lay. There were a ton of jokes and not as many uncomfortable moments as you might think, because Aria and Nancy really believe in transparency—and demonstrate it by example.

The result of this drastic effort? One of the most unique, authentic, and inspiring displays of leadership I've experienced in my professional career. Aria and Nancy displayed grace and humility, and openly discussed strengths and weaknesses. They pitched answers to our questions, and they pitched their leadership skills. Gossip eased, morale lifted, and we trusted more than ever that that Nancy and Aria had our backs.

A BIG Year: The New World

Since 2013, DoSomething has undergone a huge shift in our core product offering: we went from hosting ten or twelve campaigns annually to the big, bold vision of "Any cause, anytime, anywhere." We made the decision to host more than 250 campaigns this year alone. This awesome idea came from Mike, Head of Product. He pitched the "Everything a campaign" notion at the staff retreat last year.

> **Tweetable Takeaway**
> Let XYZers pitch—you'll be amazed by the creativity and energy you unleash.

After Mike pitched, we got down to details. The Campaigns team had to pitch ideas for 250 projects to the team and the board. The Product team had to pitch systems to host so many campaigns and to allow on-demand publishing of ideas. The Tech team had to pitch ideas to implement everything. And the Content team had to pitch the words we'd use to talk about it. It was a big year for us as an XYZ organization; everyone was an entrepreneur. There were celebrations, and there were tears and fails. But ultimately, there was major success.

If you let people in your organization pitch, you'll be amazed by the creativity and energy you unleash. And you'll be one step closer to becoming an XYZ organization.

It takes a full year of employment at DoSomething.org to experience every pitch tradition here. None of us are experts when we leave, but we've received an amazing amount of practice speaking in front of people. We've developed more confidence in our ideas and creativity, and we bring this all to our future endeavors.

Many people who leave DoSomething.org do so to pursue their own entrepreneurial venture. We're always pitching each other weird ideas to pursue outside of work—an app, a book, a robot, a bar. Working here is a springboard for startups. We get so spoiled by the level of autonomy that it becomes difficult to adjust to working in a traditional environment.

Once we leave here, we want to do more tricks! I know that I've been spoiled beyond belief—and, if I ever leave, I'm hoping one day I'll find another XYZ organization to work for. If not, I'll probably have to start one myself.

QUESTIONS TO GET YOU STARTED:

1. How do you celebrate individual wins? Do you?

2. Sometimes the loudest voice in the room wins. What are ways introverts can step up to bat in a culture of pitching?

3. Have you ever publicly admitted failure at work? What happened?

4. Do you feel positively or negatively when a leader shows vulnerability?

5. How can your office provide more public forums for pitching and innovation?

6. Is there a channel for feedback in your office?

7. When has someone from a different team influenced your decisions?

8. XYZers want to take the lead. How can you support your employees to be more entrepreneurial?

9. What are some ways to balance collaboration with individual achievements?

10. What question would you drop in a fishbowl to anonymously ask your bosses?

11. What was your last pitch?

ABOUT THE CONTRIBUTOR

Julie is Head of User Experience at DoSomething.org. She spends most of her day making wireframes for software products that support young people making an impact on their communities. She loves bikes and flowcharts and considers herself a friendly introvert. She also brews a mean pourover.

THREE

GROW YOUR STAFF OVERNIGHT

• • •

HOW TO TURN INTERNS INTO YOUR BIGGEST ASSET

Sarah Piper-Goldberg,
Campaigns Manager:
Discrimination and Bullying

At DoSomething.org, we recognize that interns are an incredibly precious resource. They are people who are passionate enough about your workplace that they've opted to spend a chunk of time with you for pennies. We know that interns are doing us a favor— not the other way around. If you can learn how to do it effectively, running an internship program can be a huge asset to your company.

When people ask me how long I've worked at DoSomething.org, I start to answer by saying, "Well, I started as an intern in 2010," but then hesitate as the person's eyes gloss over. "That's not a real job," I imagine they're thinking to themselves. "She probably just got a bunch of people coffee." Feeling compelled to counter these doubtful thoughts, I explain: I began as a Graphic Design intern on a mission to use my creative skills for good. After falling in love not only with the work I was doing but also with the culture at DoSomething, I stayed on as the Data intern and subsequently interned with the Campaigns team. I was then hired full-time as Head of Fun. In this role, among my other HR responsibilities, I actually ended up managing the entire internship program. Later, I transitioned to the Campaigns team, where I now create and run national campaigns for over two million young people to take action, and directly manage interns of my own. All of this happened over the course of just four years.

I watch the face of the person who was likely questioning the legitimacy of my internship experience change from bored to impressed as I explain this with pride.

About 25 percent of our current staff interned with us before they were hired full time. Our internship program is in-depth, fun, unique, and draws the type of people who we know are interested in working with us. The program essentially tests them as full-time staff, making it easy for our former interns to become some of our best candidates. Wouldn't you rather hire an office manager who already knows your organizational system, your corporate culture, and your staff members' last names than someone who may not know (or even care) what your dress code is? And isn't an account associate who has already researched companies' ins and outs, sat in on a pitch, or contributed to a phone call much more attractive than someone who hasn't?

Interns get it because they're already living it. And they want in. XYZ companies are smart enough to open that door.

APPLICATION PROCESS

If you don't think the sites where you post internship opportunities are important, think again. Slapping intern job descriptions on your website and waiting to see who takes the bait doesn't result in a high-quality pool of applicants. LinkedIn is a great place to start to attract professional candidates. Post on Idealist.org, a vast database for not-for-profit internship and job listings, and you'll attract potential interns who are cause focused. Posting on college boards will result in incredibly eager and excited applicants. Each platform serves a unique purpose and in turn has a unique applicant pool.

We post on all of those platforms, because we're looking for a mixture of all of those traits. Think about the types of interns you want working for you, and make it easy for them to find you.

> ### Tweetable Takeaway
> Choose where you post internship listings wisely; you'll attract different types of people depending on where you advertise the program.

What to Look For

We look for interns who are passionate about social change, have a good work ethic, and have some experience or interest in the field to which they've applied. But most of all, we're looking to learn. Every employee and every intern at an XYZ company should bring something to the team. Our interns have firsthand knowledge of the college market, of new innovations, technology, and TV shows. DoSomething.org interns are an average age of twenty-one years old, which happens to fit perfectly into our target market. We can walk up to any college intern and ask what artist is hot right now or if people still say "YOLO" before we tweet it or include it in our campaign content. We need young people in our office; they end up being our in-house focus group.

Creating a diverse team is also an important factor when hiring. Our member base over-indexes for young people of color, and we want to ensure that our intern class reflects that demographic. Brainstorms with interns should provide us with perspectives that match the audience that will eventually participate in the campaigns derived from those sessions. We're not just looking for interns who can write professional e-mails or speak eloquently in front of crowds. If they can contribute ideas about personal experiences they've had and how it has affected them, they can be a huge advantage to the team. For this reason, we interview with questions that bring to light the applicant's integrity, thought processes, and interest in DoSomething.org as a whole. Some examples (for several positions) are:

- "What do you think the voice of DoSomething.org's social media channels is trying to achieve? How does it compare to other brands you follow on social media?"
- "What's your favorite DoSomething.org campaign? How would you change the call to action to encourage more of your friends to participate?"
- "Who are the top five media outlets you'd partner with for our campaign? What kind of audience would those outlets attract?"

These questions challenge applicants to relate their real-life experiences to our audience, products, and team.

The bottom line: find interns who fit your culture. Not your aunt's second-cousin's daughter's best friend who is the niece of the man who just happens to be one of your major clients or customers. If you hire someone who has a knack for social media that your team lacks, he or she fills a void. Imagine you're running a campaign about immigration, but no one at your office has firsthand experience on the issue. If you hire a passionate guy from an immigrant family who can tell you about his real-life experience of being undocumented for the beginning of his life, he's filling a gap. You're adding to your team—not just cloning your existing staff.

Above all, we look for interns who are willing to go the extra mile—the ones who bleed our colors, and who are invested in propelling the organization forward. Not only do these enthusiastic applicants' skills match our culture and purpose, but they also understand how we work.

Our Marketing and PR intern, Diane, applied by making her own Marketing and PR "Culture Book" that included a host of relevant, youth-friendly suggestions for celebrities and marketing partners for us to work with. She highlighted cultural trends and important dates that we could use to promote campaigns (including movie release dates and something called "Hug Your Cat Day"). She even included some new campaign ideas, a task that wouldn't even fall into her day-to-day duties. She finished it off with a page on why she was a perfect fit with our culture. Obviously she was, and she made a huge impact on our organization as a whole.

Felicia applied for the Social Media intern position with a tweet that linked to a video of her lip-syncing a Janet Jackson song in her dorm room (with lyrics about her being hired as the Social Media intern dubbed over it). She got the job. Twice. She's now on our Content Team as a full-time staff member.

The creativity our program inspires is evident. We even had an applicant vie for our attention by sending someone in a chicken suit to deliver a singing telegram to our office. That creativity showcases one of the most important traits an intern can bring to an office: passion for the brand.

Tweetable Takeaway

In an XYZ company, passion and life experience can trump prerequisites. Don't overlook a candidate because his or her résumé doesn't boast tons of work experience.

Interviews

Every intern at DoSomething.org goes through an interview process similar to the one full-time applicants endure before joining the team.

The Head of Fun, who runs the internship program, establishes dates and assigns a specific number of interns to each department depending on the department size and the amount of work they'll have during that time period. This ensures that each intern will have enough real work to do and will significantly contribute to their team. It also distributes the workloads of full-time staff evenly. The Head of Fun manages the intern class as a whole and maintains the structure of the program, but staff members are ultimately responsible for managing their specific intern: assigning tasks, checking in, and making sure the intern is happy and productive. For this reason, each staff member who manages an intern is in charge of interviewing and choosing his or her specific intern. This fosters clarity of purpose, stronger relationships, and productivity.

Although each staff member should hire and manage their specific intern, there should be one staff member responsible for overseeing the entire program and intern class. The interview process generally consists of a video chat or in-person interview and potentially some follow-up "homework," depending on the type of position. We give assignments that reflect our brand and that are relevant to the position. A Backend Developer may ask to see some coding samples, while the Marketing intern applicant might be asked to name five celebrities who would be good matches for a specific campaign. This supports our tactic of seeking applicants who have the skills we're looking for, but can also demonstrate their passion and understanding for our brand.

PAYMENT

There's been a lot of talk in the media about the lack of financial compensation for interns in the workplace. Let me be clear about this one: YOU MUST PAY YOUR INTERNS! First of all, it's just not nice to exploit the free labor of hard-working people. Second, it really doesn't require that much money. We offer a $3,000 stipend for our full-time Summer Program and a $1,000 stipend for our part-time Fall and Spring Programs. If each intern isn't worth a few grand to you, maybe you should reread my first paragraph. You get what you pay for. If you offer compensation, the quality of applicants will be stronger, and your interns will take the job more seriously.

Internships should be as coveted as full-time positions. Last summer, we received nearly four thousand applications for our internship program. By emphasizing the positions' perks—real work, sense of community, opportunities for fun and learning—we're not only able to attract a self-selecting, committed, and talented group, but we also instill a sense of honor and appreciation for the position in the lucky ones who make the cut. If we offer them photocopying and coffee-fetching tasks—unpaid, menial labor—we'll attract applicants who are drawn to that work. And we don't want that type of intern.

> **Tweetable Takeaway**
>
> A paid, structured program with real work and time for fun scores you applicants who fight it out to fill each spot.

Money isn't the only way to show interns you respect them and value their work. I remember being amazed that I was encouraged, along with full-time staff, to be one of Nick Cannon's VIP guests for *America's Got Talent*. Me! An intern! Being included told me I mattered.

At DoSomething.org's twentieth birthday event, our interns were invited on stage with Hanson (a '90s dream come true). It was their third day on the job. Even being invited to simple things like holiday parties and after-work events is an important gesture. It expresses our belief that interns are a significant part of the team, not lackeys who have to go home at the end of the day because they're "too young" to hang with the full-time staff, or "not experienced enough" to shout out ideas during a brainstorm.

> **Tweetable Takeaway**
>
> Money and experiences aren't elements to neglect. If you can't "afford" to pay interns, you need to rethink your organization's structure.

ONBOARDING

We encourage interns to play by the same rules that our full-time staff follow. They undergo an orientation that's almost identical to the one we have for our full-time staff, where—among icebreakers and intros to our departments—they review and agree to the same handbook that our full-time staff sign. If they breach any of the rules in the handbook, they're out.

However, this is far from a handbook full of ridiculous regulations that we've established as booby traps for them to step in. They are easy-to-follow, basic rules that every employee can and should abide by.

For your reference, here's the table of contents for our office handbook (the starred items do not apply to interns). Hint: imitation is the sincerest form of flattery:

- Welcome
- About DoSomething
- Introductory Statement
- Equal Employment Opportunity
- Sexual Harassment
- Conflict of Interests
- Confidentiality
- Employment Categories**
- Introductory Period**
- Payroll**
- Insurance Benefits**
- Contribution of Medical/COBRA**
- Retirement Plan
- Benefits**
- Vacation Benefits**
- Holidays
- Sick Leave Benefits**
- Family or Medical Leave**
- Pregnancy Leave**
- Paternity Leave**
- Personal Time/Bereavement
- Religious Holidays
- Volunteer Sabbatical**
- Comp Time and Working from Home
- Jury Duty
- Timekeeping**
- Office Hours
- Drug and Alcohol Use
- Employee Conduct and
- Disciplinary Actions

- Terminations
- Safety
- Domestic Violence Awareness
- Dress Code
- Use of Equipment
- Staff Conferences**
- Business Travel Expenses**
- Computer and E-Mail Usage
- Space Use
- Return of Property
- Whistleblower Policy
- Employee Acknowledgment Form

At orientation, interns spend several hours in a room, huddled together with the Head of Fun learning about our organization and each other in creative ways that reflect our brand. One year they made a smoothie that symbolized their hopes for the summer individually and as a whole, and another year they all did improv together. They've already been drawn in by the job description, social media presence, and the informative short video they've watched obsessively on YouTube, but they deserve to understand what the organization is about from the inside out. They should be versed in the structure of the organization, the history, schedule, rules, and one another.

Orientation not only starts interns on the path to brand evangelism, it also encourages them to create a support system among themselves.

Interns learn the rules in orientation and sign the handbook to agree to follow those rules. But the kind of intern we strive to hire not only knows they need to be in the office from 9:30 A.M. to 5:30 P.M., they want to be there. In fact, some of our interns have shown up too early to work. I once received a call from Brad, a panicked intern who had arrived early and set off the alarm system by accident. Now that's dedication (although not advised—the NYPD was not as enthused as I was).

Of course, a few hours of sitting inside during your average corporate orientation tends to get tedious. Our solution is the Annual Intern Scavenger Hunt. During this daylong event, we split our interns into teams to run around the city and complete as many items on our challenge list as possible. The tasks aren't what you'd expect, like "eat a hot dog on 49th Street" or "travel to Yankee Stadium"; instead, the challenges are a form of love for our partners. For example, we send interns to deliver ice cream to board members and recite a love poem to a key corporate partner. These fun and memorable experiences are also the greatest onboarding exercise imaginable. In one day, our interns have met and learned the names of all our board members, bonded with key marketing partners, and familiarized themselves with our corporate partners. You can stick interns in a room and make them memorize lists of names, or you can encourage them to learn by doing. After the initial in-office orientation, the Scavenger Hunt fosters institutional knowledge through fun.

> **Tweetable Takeaway**
> Orientation doesn't have to be an endless slog through a handbook. Mix it up with fun, hands-on activities that achieve the same goals

PROGRAM

The word "program" has closely followed the word "internship" more than once in the previous sections. That was intentional. We don't just grab a handful of college kids on various liberal arts quads and stick them in a dark corner of our office for ten weeks. The interns we've hired to work with us have enrolled in an experience—a boot camp and business school rolled into one. The program has a real structure, which is what makes it a real work experience. It fosters growth and is impressive on a résumé. DoSomething.org prides itself on running efficiently—with several departments, a highly monitored budget, and real impact. And our internship program runs the same way.

We have about sixty full-time staff members at DoSomething.org. That might not seem huge, but add thirty paid college interns to that and it's a sizable organization. And our interns aren't cleaning out our supply closets and reorganizing our books; they're doing employee-level work directly alongside a full-time staff member who serves as their manager. It's a win/win situation. We're able to complete more work in less time, and the interns are doing something personally and professionally meaningful. For instance, one of our interns was trusted to choose and award a young person with a $1,000 grant each week for social change projects. That's far more important, productive, and relevant than stapling papers for an upcoming board meeting. We believe in these young people's autonomy, passion, and skills.

Tweetable Takeaway

XYZ Companies give interns real responsibility is a win/win—they'll gain work experience while lightening your staff members' workloads.

Structure

We separate our internship groups—which we call "classes"—by semesters for our part-time Fall and Spring Programs, and full-time Summer Program. We post internship listings and accept applications a few months before each program starts. The Fall and Spring Programs each run for thirteen weeks, and the interns are required to work in our office twelve to fifteen hours per week during that semester to receive the full $1,000 stipend. We're careful to fit the program into a college schedule—it starts about a week after classes begin and ends before finals start. Fall and Spring Programs mainly attract undergraduate NYC-based college students who are looking for an internship to supplement their semester.

The Summer Program runs for ten weeks, and interns receive a $3,000 stipend for working in our office full-time. Although this program attracts locals as well, more hopefuls from out of state who are looking to live out their NYC dream with us for the summer apply for this program. The Summer Program is more in-depth than the Fall and Spring Programs because all the interns are in the office at the same time (unlike the Fall and Spring interns whose hours are more dependent on their class schedules) so they have more opportunity to connect with the staff and each other. It's more than your average internship; the program is supported by supplemental programs and activities in and outside of the office.

Goals

At the beginning of the program, the Head of Fun guides each staff member in setting goals with the intern he or she is managing. In the Fall and Spring Programs, these goals consist of one long-term project and one personal project or skill set. The manager assesses what will be the most important tasks or skills to work on for the semester and figures out a way to make them interesting for the intern. Priorities change, and these goals aren't set in stone; however, they help the managers keep track of what their interns are working on and keep the interns working toward something.

The Summer Program goals are more in-depth because the Summer interns are with us for ten full-time, consecutive weeks. We ask each of the interns and their managers to come up with three personal goals and three DoSomething.org goals that focus on the organization. Some of the goals that a former Summer Campaigns intern specializing in physical and mental health included:

DoSomething.org Goals:

1. Understand the campaign models and process from start to finish.
2. Brainstorm and flesh out a few campaign ideas after understanding the models and process.
3. Apply my public health background to create research briefs on health issues we haven't run campaigns around yet.
4. Help form and communicate with the physical health and mental health advisory councils.

Personal Goals:

1. Help with a video. Meet with [the video manager] to see an entire video process through (planning, filming, editing).
2. Learn more about how texting and SMS gaming impact and promote behavior change and action around an issue (and hopefully find an idea for my master's thesis). Meet with [the Mobile team] to discuss mobile process—and maybe [the Data team] to review data from previous mobile games we've done.
3. Learn how marketing partnerships are developed for the different campaigns. Meet with [the Marketing team] to see how this process works. Also attend Marketing meetings for current campaigns to see how that process works.

> **Tweetable Takeaway**
>
> Set intern—and employee—goals to keep everyone on task, help managers delegate work, and make it easier to assess success.

Open All Doors

Because we value our interns, we never make them fetch us coffee. We include them in brainstorms. We invite them to meetings outside the office with partners. We treat them like people—not minions!

As we described in the first chapter, the DoSomething.org office has an open layout. Interns sit at communal desks right in the middle of all the action. This setup compels them to bond with each other while giving them an all-access pass to staff. They see and hear everything that goes on, and often act as a staff member pit stop between desk and kitchen or bathroom.

> **Tweetable Takeaway**
>
> House interns in a central space or closer to their managers. They'll feel valued, learn more, and provide a nearby focus group for staff.

Interns are invited to all meetings. We encourage them to sit in on brainstorms, contribute to pitches outside the office, and speak up on conference calls with partners. We know that fresh, passionate eyes are a good thing. We welcome their questions, and if an intern is sitting quietly in a brainstorm, one of the staff will often solicit his or her opinion. Interns are there to learn, produce, and contribute. The only way to do this well is to make sure they're included in everything.

One of our Campaigns interns, Pam, was thrown into a project at the last minute because her manager was out of the office. It became her job to organize young people in the Philadelphia area to reach out to their governor and plead to save music education as a part of our Band Together campaign. Having participated in all of the meetings and planning for the campaign, Pam was able to cover for her manager seamlessly. When the entire staff was out of the office for our annual retreat, the interns ran it in our absence. We assigned "captains" to take charge of maintaining the space and locking the doors, and we trusted the interns to manage the office and continue working toward their goals. They did all of this and more; they even took over the DoSomething .org Twitter account while we were gone, tweeting out updates with the hashtag #internsruntheoffice.

Tweetable Takeaway

Include your interns in meetings. The more they know, the more helpful they are to you.

We don't just value our interns within the walls of our office or behind closed doors. They aren't our "secret weapons"; we trust them to represent our brand in public, too. Several of our interns accompany, or even replace, staff at external events. A former intern, Teresa, attended an award show in her manager's place because her manager knew Teresa was interested in celebrity journalism. It's that access and opportunity for growth that keeps interns engaged in an XYZ Company.

It's important that these contributors are not just known as "John's intern" or "the one with the bangs." We take the time to learn each intern's name, not just the names of the interns we manage or the interns who work with our team. Would you want to be known as the intern who always brings egg salad for lunch—or as Emily, the smart one whose idea became an actual marketing initiative?

Allow Them to Explore

Our interns attend meetings with their managers, listen, learn, and share ideas. But what if the Marketing intern wants to learn about product creation? Simple: we let her sit in on a Product team meeting so that she can gain a holistic understanding of the organization. We've had interns who learned to code, shoot PSAs, and pitch companies all in one summer—all of whom weren't necessarily hired to do any of those things. DoSomething.org interns can leave their internship with us as the Marketing intern and add that experience to their résumé along with knowledge of basic HTML. Learning a new skill from a meeting or one-on-one time with a full-time staff member is a form of compensation. Giving an intern the chance to learn QuickBooks or Photoshop means you've given that person a new marketable skill, something to add to his or her résumé. Those lessons are challenges as well as benefits!

Tweetable Takeaway

Allow interns to explore their interest in other departments. It's a free way to invest in them.

Interns also have some responsibilities that full-time staff don't. We split the summer intern class up into different social committees—ranging from selecting and running the biweekly bake-offs to conceptualizing and designing our Culture Book, a document that displays and defines our office culture. It may seem counterintuitive for interns, who have probably only been at the organization for a few weeks or months, to make the book that defines our culture for a whole year—but it's not. They're immersed in our culture every day, and are so eager to leave a legacy that they'll nail the assignment.

Tweetable Takeaway

Allow interns to own projects and learn new skills. It frees up full-time staff and deepens their investment in your brand.

Check-Ins

We gather our intern class weekly for an "all hands on deck" check-in, moderated by the Head of Fun. Each intern shares an accomplishment, a goal, and a request, just like staff members do at our weekly staff meeting. This formula is a terrific way for the Head of Fun to spot any intern who might be stuck or losing focus, and an excellent way for interns to learn about other roles in the office and develop mutual respect. Nancy likes to join this meeting, as it gives her a chance listen to the interns and share her accomplishments, goals, and requests.

We know interns are eager to dive in and help out in any way they can; however, we don't expect them to be experts right off the bat. Managers set up weekly check-ins to talk through what's on the table for that week and if there is anything that might get in the way of achieving that. During the Summer Program, the Head of Fun also meets with each intern midway through the program to ensure he or she is on the right track in terms of following the program. It's also a chance to talk about anything that the intern doesn't feel comfortable discussing with his or her manager. Managing interns, answering their questions, and facilitating their growth is just as important as anything else we do.

Interns are not the only ones who benefit from mentoring and skill building. Staff members who manage interns gain a lot from the process as well. Many of the DoSomething.org full-time staff members are young. Most have never managed someone before and may not be in a position where managing a full-time staff member is in their immediate future. Managing an intern, especially one with so much responsibility, is a significant task. It forces staff to hone new skills and serves as a really great trial run in management.

Allow Time for Fun

For our staff, summer means interns. It's almost like the rest of the year is a placeholder until we have our real full-time staff of eighty or more—and it kind of makes every summer feel like freshman year of college. We go to social events, play awkward icebreaker games—then look back three months later and can't believe we ever lived without each other. Our interns entertain us, challenge us, and refresh us. They don't just add to the space. They define it.

We want people to be excited about being here—and not just because we're making real change (although that's a bonus). An intern who, as a part of his or her job, has dance parties and bake-offs and sings karaoke probably doesn't see the not-for-profit sector as stuffy and traditional.

Perhaps an intern spends some time talking to a staff member instead of finishing up that file you need sorted. The file isn't sorted—but they have a conversation with your COO they'll never forget. That access and those extra perks are investments in your company. Your interns are much more likely to talk about that conversation than about file

sorting with their friends and family—which in turn engages their networks in your brand and your product. One summer, our interns and staff learned a coordinated dance (flash mob–style) to Katy Perry's "Firework" for Nancy's birthday (she LOVED it). The dance was mainly led by interns—and to this day, when that song comes on, I bet you they remember the dance moves, and when their friends give them bizarre looks while they dance, they're proud to explain why they still remember the choreography.

Interns can also provide an "in" to the brands and organizations your company loves and wants to work with. Last summer, we reached out to nine other terrific not-for-profits in New York City and created a speaker series together. Every Wednesday night, interns from all nine organizations gathered together for pizza and beer, and the CEO of one organization spoke and fielded questions. The interns were exposed to different leadership styles and different companies and were able to meet each other in one place. It was fun, informative, and cheap—and a smart way to cultivate future intern and employee applicants.

An intern immersed in your culture is far more beneficial than one who is drowning in work. You have staff to run the day-to-day operations of your organization full time. What you want the most out of these interns is an undying passion for your company and brand.

> **Tweetable Takeaway**
> If you invest in your interns' growth, you'll turn them into some of your best brand ambassadors.

POST-INTERNSHIP

A good internship doesn't end when the work is done. Your company is likely your interns' first employment experience, one that will be listed on their LinkedIn profile for years to come. Former interns become lifelong brand ambassadors. They talk about their experience to their friends, siblings, great-aunts, and current employers. If their experience was a good one, this is great—and free advertising. Former interns have sent us new corporate partners and donors, job applicants, advice, and chocolate. These people know you, your brand, your pain points, and your strengths—why lose them after ten great weeks? Instead, keep them as a virtual focus group, recruiting tool, and marketing machine. You never know whom your interns know—they could end up becoming more connected than you are! Keep that in mind while you're interacting with them during and after their internship. You want them to excitedly tell their friends, family, and perhaps future investors or partners as loudly as possible that they have interned with an amazing company.

Keep in Contact

At the end of the internship program, our Head of Fun creates and sends out a survey that's optional but strongly encouraged. It's a great time to get candid feedback about your program. Following are a few examples of questions we ask in our survey:

- How did you hear about DoSomething.org?
- Is there anything you wish you'd known before the internship started?
- What's one piece of advice you'd give to incoming interns?
- If you could change one thing about the program, what would it be?
- Were you satisfied with the application and interview processes? If not, how would you have changed the processes?
- How do you feel about the amount of guidance and direction you received from your supervisor?

The last question of the survey asks for a personal e-mail address so we can add it to our e-mail list of former interns. We use these to send invites, post job descriptions, and solicit feedback on ideas. We keep in touch with DoSomething.org interns through several other channels:

1. Facebook. The Head of Fun creates intern class–specific Facebook groups after the internship is over. The Head of Fun can simply invite all of our former interns to our office party or post a request for volunteers for an event we're running and receive an immediate response.
2. Annual events. Interns know they are invited to our holiday party each year, which has become a reunion for many past intern classes.
3. LinkedIn. It's a good idea to post a reference or endorsement of an intern as soon as the internship is complete. They might not need a reference for a few years, but it's smart for you to complete it

while you still remember them and the impact that he or she had. It's worth connecting on LinkedIn and possibly even starting a group, open to current and former interns.

Tweetable Takeaway

Conduct a post-internship survey. It shows interns that you value their opinions and provides you with feedback to improve your program.

Or, Hire Them

Last summer we were going through some restructuring and expansion of our Tech and Product teams, but we weren't looking for a traditional User Experience (UX) designer. So we brought an intern named Luke on board to be our Graphic Design/User Experience intern. He ended up showing us not only how extremely talented he was, but that we did desperately need a UX designer. Luke's day-to-day contributions and smart, clear, visually appealing presentations in our staff meetings led us to offer him a full-time position as a UX designer that started right after he graduated. By hiring Luke, we brought someone onto the team who knew our staff and work style, but who also introduced us to a new skill set we didn't even know we needed.

It may seem like a bit of a risk to hire an intern who doesn't have much experience; and of course, this isn't how you'd fill your COO position. After five semesters of devoted interning, karaoke singing, and bonding with the staff, DoSomething.org hired me full time as the person who does the hiring and culture keeping, even though I'd never hired anyone in my life. It was my first full-time job, but since I had lived and breathed DoSomething.org for so long, it was a good fit. When I started, I wasn't entirely sure how I was going to do it, but several full-time hires and intern classes later, I had figured it out.

Despite my nervousness about this new step, I asked for even more responsibility before accepting the offer. I told Nancy that I wanted to manage the internship program as well. I just couldn't imagine watching someone else manage the process that had allowed me to grow personally and professionally. I felt like it was my intern rite of passage to bring other interns into the world that I had come to know and love. And she went for it.

Tweetable Takeaway

Interns' prior knowledge paired with experience at your organization makes them valuable assets to your full-time team.

IN SUMMARY

Five years and some change after my first day in the DoSomething.org office—nervously hoping the too-good-to-be-true internship description would become a reality—I've had the opportunity to work in several departments, from Design to Data to HR to Campaigns. If I hadn't initially been drawn in by the fun yet purpose-driven internship description on Idealist.org, I would never have had any of these opportunities.

The in-depth onboarding orientation allowed me to quickly adjust to the office environment and begin to create a strong bond with my fellow interns and full-time staff members. My managers always treated me as a fellow staff member, giving me the same level of work they were completing, inviting me to eat lunch with them the team, but I also received an extra level of help or motivation if I needed it. I was learning by doing.

This type of training helped me to feel more confident in my full-time position managing entire classes of interns during the summer, spring, and fall. I understood the importance of an accurate and detailed job description, the interview process, in-depth onboarding, and close management that left room for independent work. I also brought that experience and mind-set to interns whom I managed directly when I joined the Campaigns team. I was more attentive to my interns' needs and interests—holding check-ins and making sure the work he or she was doing was meaningful and interesting—than I would have been if I hadn't been an intern myself. DoSomething .org's XYZ mind-set makes it so that we don't just pay attention to the behaviors of our target market during the campaigns we run or the usability of our website; it also comes to light during our internship program. This model allows our staff and interns learn to read our audience from the inside out.

I'm proof that a good internship can shape your entire career. I was given an incredible opportunity to explore with guidance and be included in a fantastic team. At the same time, I was encouraged to create my own relationships and experiences, and take ownership over real work in a bottom-up environment. I was able not only to utilize these skills within the DoSomething.org office, but I can take them with me throughout my entire professional career and personal life.

QUESTIONS TO GET YOU STARTED

1. Do you have a built-out internship program? If so, do you create specific job descriptions for interns?

2. Where do you post the internship openings? How do you recruit for interns—and what does it say about your priorities?

3. What are you hoping to learn or achieve from your interns?

4. How do your staff and interns keep track of the work the interns are doing? Do you set goals or benchmarks?

5. Who manages each intern? Who manages the program as a whole?

6. Where do your interns sit? Are they in a dark corner brewing your coffee, or are they right in the middle of the office, interacting with one another and your full-time staff?

7. What is the bright-line rule for including or not including your interns?

8. Are you paying your interns? Are you giving them any other benefits?

9. Can you name all of the interns in your office or department?

10. Do you maintain contact with former interns? How?

11. If you were an intern at your company, would you brag to your friends about your experience?

ABOUT THE CONTRIBUTOR

Sarah Piper-Goldberg creates and runs campaigns about bullying and discrimination at DoSomething.org. She received an associate of arts from Bard College at Simon's Rock and a bachelor of fine arts from Parsons the New School for Design. Sarah has always been inspired by design, campaigns, and products that broaden perspectives and promote empathy, understanding, and advocacy. Sarah would like to thank her two cats, Sigmund Freud and Franz Kafka, for giving up their coveted sleeping spots on the computer keyboard so she could write this chapter.

FOUR

BEING DATA-INFORMED

• • •

WHY MEASUREMENT IS ESSENTIAL

Jeff Bladt, Chief Data Officer

Think about the way your body's nervous system compels you to respond to touching a hot stove by mistake: you move your hand as quickly as possible. Your organization has a similar kind of nervous system: a nearly real-time feedback loop that can inform the efficacy of programs, products, and services. Unfortunately, most companies don't tap into this. If they receive the information, they either don't know how to react or aren't empowered to maneuver a quick enough reaction. This chapter aims to remedy that.

INTRODUCTION TO THE DOT.ORGANISM— A DATA-INFORMED ORGANIZATION

When I think about the word organization, I conjure associations with bureaucracy and hierarchy, of org charts and five-year plans. And most data out there supports this sense of the organization as a fairly rigid structure. The top Google autocomplete for the term "organizations are" is "considered static systems."

However, the work that DoSomething.org and its three million members are committed to doesn't match this sense of an "organization." The way we function, interact, and learn with our members is completely different. We are not a static system with a detailed plan; rather, we're a distributed network of members who communicate with our small team in hundreds of different ways.

We have just sixty full-time employees centered in Manhattan who support those three million members—which is roughly one old person per every fifty thousand young people. That's a huge differential—one that means that we simply cannot approach our organization in the traditional, hierarchical way. In order for DoSomething.org to scale, we must be nimble and fluid. We leverage technology and capitalize on the data opportunities inherent in doing so to grow and support our membership. Other dot.org's have arrived here as well. Donors Choose, Kiva, and Change.org are a few of these distributed networks maintained by small passionate staff that have an on-the-ground impact on millions of lives.

To return to the analogy of the hand and the hot stove top, our nervous systems send real-time feedback to our mind and muscles to move, NOW! In much the same way, a distributed network of our members uses a technology-enabled platform to provide us with constant feedback. As a result, we have an organic, reactive system, with users spread out across the country. Every initiative that we offer, SMS broadcast, social media post, search on our site, and countless other interactions are opportunities for our members to tell us, "Yes, we want more opportunities like this," or "Ugh, that's not really what we're looking for." I call this organization of our members and staff a dot.organism.

Tweetable Takeaway

XYZ Companies use communications with members and customers as opportunities for feedback.

DoSomething.org has a data team that follows a simple underlying philosophy: our members are our nervous system. Whether nonprofit or corporate, XYZ organizations must view their members and participants as valuable sources of information on how well their programs or products are received—or not. Unfortunately, 83 percent of nonprofits don't have someone in charge of measuring the impact of their actions.

Three Principles of the Dot.organism

I like to define the dot.organism in terms of three principles:

1. Empathy. You must know what success looks like for your members and your organization. Utilize data to solve member

problems, not create new ones. This starts with qualitative feedback and testing.

2. Focus. If you use data smartly, you can distinguish between data and metrics and create KPIs (key performance indicators) that foster long-term organizational health. These metrics are tools to find organizational bright spots (as well as areas with low return on investment).

3. Speed. The speed of your insights must match the speed of your decision making.

Building a Data Organization

What should you do to build a data organization? Data culture needs to be top-down; management needs to be on board.

Your new dot.organism will need to take advantage of the revolution in culture that comes with being data-informed. Management should support this orientation and prioritization of data from the top.

Data Evolution in Your Organization

Organizations that become more aware of data move through several phases of development. They usually start out not bothering to measure or track anything; sometimes they've spent years relying on strong intuition and direct, informal feedback. As these groups develop and use more sophisticated ways of providing information and access to services, they have a lot more potential to quantify and record their activities and to harness this information for strategic purposes. Where is your organization in the following four phases?

1. The "Pre-Data" Phase. It's entirely possible for new or small organizations to operate without tracking or quantifying actions. Having fewer employees makes it easy to keep abreast of organizational processes, and the founder is often very involved in all aspects of the operation. Her intuition and inspiration guide decision making, and she spends the little time she has outside of daily operations pitching the organization's dream to others. Any data desired would have to be pulled together on an ad hoc basis.

2. The "Informal" Data Phase. In this phase, data collection is ad hoc and performed by multiple individuals. It's difficult to compare

persons, departments, or information over time, and large swaths of data tend to be ignored or categorized with vague metrics. As a result, decision making is still driven by intuition and loose guesses.

For example, a social media team might be obsessed with Twitter followers, whereas a program director might focus on the results of a satisfaction survey e-mailed out to event participants. This level of attention to data represents marked improvement over not measuring anything; however, this casual approach can sometimes be less helpful. It's dangerous to assume, "All our responses have been positive, so we are running the right programs." It is just as likely that survey questions are leading or that positive responses are masking a decrease in scope. Isolated data collection methods like these also don't work toward organizational values or mission. The same actions that lead to more social media followers might also be diminishing the brand's stature.

Another hiccup: the first areas that can quantify their actions are often the first to get more funding—even if they're the ones who need it the least. Consider social media tools, an area where numerous expensive suites of analytics tools are available but add limited value.

Always spend more on staff than on fancy technology or tools. A good rule of thumb: for every ninety dollars spent on staff, spend no more than ten on tools and software. One driven analyst right out of college is more valuable than similarly priced enterprise analytics packages.

Tweetable Takeaway

For every $10 you spend on data software, spend $90 on staffing.

3. The "Data Agnostic/Data Antagonistic" Phase. By this point, several parts of the organization are rigorously and consistently collecting data. Some metrics and corresponding goals have been defined, but a "data culture" doesn't exist—yet, at least. Those setting the goals and those counting the beans don't share

information or pay grade. People still make major decisions based on their gut or "because it has worked before/elsewhere" logic.

Though the way it collects data is similar to data agnostic organizations, the antagonistic organization is different because it has actionable data—but ignores or subverts it. Senior and established decision makers might see data as a threat—and therefore don't act in accordance with it.

4. The "Data-Informed/Data-Driven" Phase. Organizations that have made it here have overcome the obstacles of the preceding phases and arrived at this data culture sweet spot. You have quality metrics that represent your organizational values. Staff asks, "What do the data say?" as a matter of course, from the board down to entry-level employees. Inefficiencies are ferreted out fast and opportunities are located and acted upon.

Being data-informed is a fragile equilibrium. It is easy to lapse back to data agnosticism or to progress too far and become obsessed with the numbers. If all the numbers are up and to the left, but no one feels good about the health of the organization, then something is wrong. If there's so much to gain from becoming data-informed, why are so few organizations embracing this chance? It's likely because this approach displaces intuition and "just because" thinking. In addition, quantifying success and failure makes what seemed to be impossible comparisons now possible—and perhaps even overwhelming. Which conference has trained the best program directors? Does anyone actually read our newsletter? And if so, does this make them more likely to buy anything? Each of these questions ties back to real work being produced by real teams of qualified professionals. Despite the obvious benefits of finding bright spots to magnify, this data-informed approach will likely shed a light on the not-so-bright spots.

This is precisely why creating a data culture happens most smoothly when it starts from the top down. Employees need to know that data is not exclusively about measuring outputs but also about process. When done right, quality metrics, reported on in a timely fashion, reduce the instances and severity of failure.

Knowing the Data Skeptics

Roughly speaking, there are four types of employees in any organization.

1. Highly perceived, high performing
2. Highly perceived, low performing
3. Lowly perceived, high performing
4. Lowly perceived, low performing

One would assume that the top group (high-high) would be the easy data converts; of course, your all-stars want the best tools and analysis at their disposal. However, this isn't always how it goes; in fact, the high-highs are the most likely to be data skeptical. Quantifying their domain and performance offers little upside. They are doing quality work, and everyone agrees. Adding hard metrics can, at best, affirm this narrative and, at worst, undermine the good thing they have going. They fear— understandably so—that the outputs used to measure their performance will not fully capture the true value of their contributions. This skepticism is especially strong in any workplace where attribution is difficult (think marketing).

However, with a little effort, you can bring this group around. Taking them into the fold early, allowing them to help create new metrics, and giving them space to push back can ensure against the perception that data culture is forced on them.

Your main challenge lies next down the list: the high-lows. These are your data antagonistics. Everybody loves them, but deep down they always fear they will be found out. Their ideas are occasionally fantastic, but too often they are just shooting in the dark. They're never sure why things go right, and they instinctively turn to hide-covering mode when things go wrong. Quantifying their work only has a downside.

Outing low-performing employees and practices is the flip side of finding bright spots. After this group, you have the low-highs: your biggest champions. They have toiled too long on the lower parts of the totem. Giving these overachieving, underappreciated employees the information and framework to make their work comparable, to allow their true value to be understood, provides only an upside. These are your human bright spots.

Give this group early wins. They will love you for it and help promote your cause. And senior management will be impressed. "Look at this data! Those employees over in team X are doing great work, and we never would have known this before!"

And this brings us to the last group, the low-lows. They aren't going to fight data culture. Or embrace it. They'll simply turn their heads ten degrees and think, huh? Data?

THE DATA BALANCE

Although effective decision making starts by asking, "What do the data say?" it should not end there. Data cannot tell you what to measure, or help you decide what your end goals should be. Numbers can help you spot opportunities, but they cannot generate bold new ideas. Moreover, as soon as you start measuring something, the expectation is that it should go up. And if it doesn't, it is easy to write it off as a failure.

Overreliance on data can stifle innovation. One of DoSomething .org's most successful campaigns is Pregnancy Text, an SMS-based experience that allows young people to send a "virtual text baby" to a friend. The baby sends the recipient mildly irritating (and sometimes humorous) text messages at random intervals throughout the day, mimicking the experience of being a young parent. All the data we had prior to launching this campaign told us it would be a huge failure. Members had responded negatively to unsolicited, push messages like this every time we had tried similar campaigns in the past. Each time, we would lose far more members than we would gain. I remember when I first heard the idea, I was dead set against it; I was positive it would cost us thousands of members.

The data-driven organization would have killed Pregnancy Text right there. We had looked at the data, and the data said no. But the data-informed organization would have taken this information alongside the fervor from the campaign lead, who was clear and enthusiastic about the idea and was able to rally others in the organization. Clearly, employee excitement must count for something, even if we can't quantify it. We therefore decided to invest development time in building a demo of the campaign to test with thirty-five members.

(Oh, a side note: the data-antagonistic org would have simply played the hunch and launched the risky campaign to over one million young people.)

We were looking at a small sample; therefore, if we only considered quantifiable aspects of member engagement, we'd have ended up with an incomplete and potentially misleading take on the campaign. So we talked with the members that demoed the experience. And, against all prior predictions, they actually wanted more unstructured messaging. And they were sharing the experience at rates we had not seen before.

Tweetable Takeaway

If the data conflicts with your gut, test it on a small sample.

The campaign went on to be the biggest of the year. Over half the participants in Pregnancy Text were invited by friends to try it out. It was exactly the type of idea DoSomething.org values, but which the data hadn't supported.

Being bold doesn't mean being careless. It means giving big ideas a chance.

Avoid Being Encumbered by Data

More is not always better when it comes to metrics and data. The number of key insights that organizations are seeking is a relatively static set. Adding more data is often similar to increasing the size of the haystack, while still searching for the same number of needles.

No matter how much you collect, data are useless if you aren't even going to look at the results.

Knowing When to Say No

At DoSomething.org, reports on the success of our broadcast messaging started as requests that came about every month or so and that were manually pulled from the raw data. Then, as the messaging team became more data hungry, the reports' granularity and scope grew, along with the desired frequency. Eventually, the reports were coming on a weekly basis. The ability of the messaging team to use the reports for strategic messaging was great. Engagement was up and complaints down. But the time needed for our analyst Bob to generate the reports only mounted. Soon, Bob was spending five hours a week to keep up with the messaging team's appetite, eating into the time he had to tackle other requests.

Eventually, weekly reporting was put on hold. The forty hours needed to remove the analyst from the process was invested, and now instead of five hours a week, the Data team spends one hour a month reviewing it with the content team.

Metrics versus Data

One afternoon last fall, a cheer suddenly spread through the DoSomething.org offices. A newly released video featuring well-known YouTube comedians asking young people to donate their used sports equipment to youths in need had received over 1.5 million views. It was twice as popular as any video to date. Success!

Then came the data report: only eight viewers had signed up to donate equipment.

The celebration stopped. Nothing had changed; the video still had 1.5 million views. But we were forced to face a hard truth: companies must decide which numbers matter. This is what separates metrics from data.

Metrics are buckets that contain data. And a successful organization can only carry so many buckets. Metrics tie to an organization's definition of success: for DoSomething.org, success is social change. In the case above, success meant donations, not video views—which unfortunately meant that the campaign was not the success we originally assumed it had been.

What Is a Metric?

We can't control our data, but we can control what we care about—and what we care about drives organizational change. Good data analysts know that analyzing the data is the easy part. The hard part is deciding which data to analyze.

Metrics are measurements that your organization decides are important; however, just because something is important does not mean it's a good metric. Good metrics are (1) quick and cost-effective to measure and (2) can be managed to. Let's use brand awareness as an example. Most organizations would readily agree that they care about customers' knowledge of their products and services. However, it's tricky to measure this awareness. You need a representative sample of the population that includes people who have never heard of your organization, because this is the one set of people about whom you are guaranteed to not have preexisting data. After efforts to gauge awareness, the direct managerial implications are murky. Changes in awareness are typically slow, making mid and short-term strategy hard to evaluate. Better metrics in our example would be measurements that approximate aware-ness that can be tracked daily or weekly, such as new member acquisi-tion, year-over-year sales growth, and so forth.

Tweetable Takeaway
Metrics are a manifestation of organizational goals. A good metric is (1) measured easily and (2) can be managed.

Other well-meaning metrics do a disservice by unintentionally creating misleading incentives for management and employees that run contrary to an organization's core principles. If you target anything that can be expressed as a simple division equation (almost all percentage or "increase/decrease" rate-of-change metrics) as something to measure, you risk encouraging the wrong behavior. Although the goal may be to increase the numerator (increased conversion rates, decreased churn, and so on), managers should always be aware of the possibility of increasing rates by decreasing the denominator. For example, if I'm selling sweaters at a retail store and want to increase the average sales per customer, I could either sell more sweaters to each customer, or sell the same number of sweaters to fewer customers! Both events would increase my average sales per customer—which is our metric in this example—and might make me look better to my manager. However, losing customers would be the wrong takeaway!

This emphasizes the importance of our point: "You can't pick your data, but you must pick your metrics." In baseball, for example, every team has the same goal—winning the World Series. Winning requires one main asset: good players. But what makes a good player? Therein lies the challenge and the purpose of metrics—defining "good players." Player evaluation used to depend on a handful of simple metrics like batting average and runs batted in (RBIs) and on managers' gut feelings about players. Then the sabermetric revolution through Billy Bean and his team of statisticians, as shown in the movie *Moneyball*, brought new metrics onto the field.

Keep in mind that all metrics are proxies for what ultimately matters (in the case of baseball, a combination of championships and profitability), and some metrics are better than others. The metrics led Bean and others to make better decisions about how to value a team's players because they more closely correlated with the ultimate goal: winning games. The data has never changed; the way we review data has. As a result, teams' strategies for winning are informed by the metrics each manager prioritizes.

This brings us to our second important point: "Organizations become their metrics."

Metrics are what you measure. And if you don't measure something, you can't manage to it. A critical question in baseball is: how impactful is a player when he steps up to the plate? One way to measure is hits. A better option turned out to be a combination of total bases (slugging) and on-base percentage (which includes hits and walks), also known as "OPS." The consequences of choosing an inferior metric trickle down. Players on teams that focused on batting average walked less, with no offsetting gains in hitting. In short, players were playing to the metrics their management valued.

The same can happen in a workplace. Measure YouTube views?

Your employees will strive for YouTube views. Measure downloads of a product? You'll get more of that. But if your actual goal is to boost sales or acquire members, better measures might be return on investment (ROI), on-site conversion, or spread—that is, do people who download the product keep using it, or share it with others? If not, all the downloads in the world won't make any difference.

Think of metrics as a filter for data: they tell you what matters in that vast sea of information. We speak in the business world about the difference between vanity and meaningful metrics. Vanity metrics are like weeds—some of them, like dandelions, might look pretty to you, but they don't do anything for your property value. Some of the most common vanity metrics in the digital world might include website visitors per month, Twitter followers, Facebook fans, and media impressions. If these metrics go up, they might drive up sales of your product. But can you prove it? If yes, great; measure away. But if you can't drive change in your organization, those metrics aren't valuable.

Which brings us to our final point: metrics are only valuable if you can manage to them.

Metrics that are costly to collect (e.g., the opinions of people who don't already know of your product) or are not available in a timely manner (e.g., comparisons to outside data sets) routinely disappoint.

And there is often little correlation between the number of viewers of something and tangible results for our organizations. For us, we've found that quality matters.

We can't control our data, but we can control what we care about—and that is what will motivate change throughout our organization. If DoSomething's metric on the YouTube video had been views, we would have called it a huge success—when, in fact, we wrote it off as a failure. That doesn't mean we won't make any more videos ever; but for now, we'll be spending our time elsewhere, collecting data on metrics that matter.

HUMANIZING DATA

Every morning, our computers greet us with an updated data report containing over 350 million data points that track various aspects of our organization's performance. Our daily challenge is to translate this haystack of information into guidance for staff, whether it's choosing the right headline for today's e-mail blast (should we ask our members to "take action" or "learn more"?) or the purpose of our summer volunteer campaign (food donation drive or recycling campaign?). In short, we are tasked with humanizing data.

When many people hear "Big Data" they often think "big brother"—that is, the one who's watching you. Big Data invokes feelings of anxiety—particularly, that being human is something computers can't track or quantify.

This fear is well founded. As the cost of collecting and storing data continues to decrease, the volume of raw data an organization has available to analyze can become overwhelming. Consider that 90 percent of data in existence was created in the last ten years.

Organizations inundated by data to analyze can lose sight of the difference between what's "significant" and what's important.

Successful use of Big Data requires putting it all into a human context by asking a simple question: whom are you trying to reach and what do you want them to do? Data give you the what; humanizing the data is needed to figure out the why. The best business decisions come about when you take a data-informed approach combined with intuition in a human context. This not only provides the best insights (analysis that accounts for intangible values), but also enables your organization to act on the information arising from data analysis.

For DoSomething.org, mapping our communications data provides an amazing window into our audience's lives. We have hundreds of data points for our over three million members—information on what and how they respond to new volunteer opportunities via e-mail and texting. There are several ways to go from 350 million data points to organizational change.

1. Look for data that could have an impact on the performance of your organization's key metric(s). Our goal is the largest number of young people making the biggest possible impact. So when we did a deep dive on our data last fall, we started with the question: Which of our members currently volunteer the most, and how can we find more people like them? Using that question allowed us to ignore certain sets of data up front (social media data and huge swaths of Google analytics) and conduct a more thorough search on what really mattered.

2. Present results in a way that makes insights intuitive to grasp for everyone in the organization. Hint: never show a regression analysis or a plot from R. In fact, very few actual numbers ended up in our final presentation on member engagement. Instead, we visualized data to find trends: even data analysts are much better at discovering geographic (and underlying demographic)!

   Presenting the data visually allowed the entire staff to quickly grasp it and contribute to the conversation. Everyone could easily see areas of high and low engagement, which led to a big insight: someone outside the analytics team noticed that members in border towns in Texas were much more engaged than members in coastal cities in the Northwest.

3. Recommend organizational actions based on the data. Once we saw who our most engaged members were, we could go back and see what campaigns those members like best. We got our answer: campaigns around improving community health, an issue that disproportionately affects minority communities. This information allows us to better tailor our volunteer campaigns going forward, reach out to the right partnerships for those campaigns, and also highlight a potential area for growth—white, male college students in the Northwest.

   Good data analysis will always require human context and insight. Connecting data to people increases the chance that data-derived insights will lead to smart organizational decisions. Moreover, by making the data more accessible, you have also increased the number of employees who can provide that breakthrough insight.

Tweetable Takeaway
Make data more accessible by attaching human insight and context.

FOCUS AND SPEED

When many organizations consider data, they think about it in the sense of evaluation—of looking at what they've already done and determining what, if any, success they had. Data are primarily a tool to placate funders, to demonstrate to them that money was spent prudently. Data are collected informally, which is to say, for a one-time use.

The speed of your insights needs to match the speed of your decision making. Good data analysis doesn't need to be reactive or slow. If you are sending out weekly e-mail updates to your members, it does you little good to receive a quarterly report on the efficacy of your messaging. Even getting a report the day after sending the message does not insulate against content falling flat. If anything, it encourages playing it safe: "We're looking at performance tomorrow, so I better send out a message today that I am sure will not underperform."

The ideal situation is to test ideas before sending them out to everyone. And most modern content and broadcast systems allow for this type of testing. Imagine that instead of playing it safe, you enabled your content writers to try out their five best ideas (within the constraints of what you would ever send out—see rules for good testing below) to just 5 or 10 percent of membership, see how they perform, and then send the best out to everyone.

We test messaging weekly at DoSomething.org, a move that's increased positive engagement three times and reduced negative engagement (in this case, members leaving DS) twofold. We've saved hundreds of thousands of members and dollars, all while greatly magnifying our campaigns' positive impact—allowing us to reach more youths and have a bigger impact.

PROCESS VERSUS OUTCOMES

Rigorous application of data insights allows employees to "fail successfully." They're no longer evaluated solely on their outputs, but also on their adherence to sound, data-informed decision making. What kinds of processes should you run? Consider the following.

Testing

Once you've achieved cultural buy-in, determined solid and representative metrics, and identified reliable data-capture strategies, you are ready to employ the next level of data-informed decision making: testing.

At every decision point that brushes against the unknown, reasonable people can and will disagree. What should we call this new product? No preexisting data will give you an exact answer; some serve as jumping-off points in approaching a solution. But ultimately, you will need to test a set of quality, data-informed ideas to determine the best path forward. To this end, there are two different types of digital testing: content and platform.

Content Testing

Content testing occurs when you have debate surrounding what text, images, and visual treatment are appropriate for a given offering. They can be as simple as trying different subject lines for e-mail newsletters and as complex as trying different tones of voice in a product description. The point is, you cannot know what will perform the best—and what works best once may not work best a second time. This is why testing content is not a quest to discover perfect messaging; rather, it's an ongoing process. To successfully test, an organization must develop and adhere to a process. Content testing is about finding the best instances within a larger framework.

Platform Testing

Platform tests move beyond interchangeable elements of content. They address larger decisions around brand, structure, and values. Repeat elements (e.g., site navigation, button size), brand choices (e.g., logo, color scheme), and nomenclature are all platform tests. This differs from content testing because you are no longer looking for short-term maximums, but rather long-term guidance.

Analysis should not all be easy and on demand. Involved and data-informed deep dives can produce large dividends. But they require departmental bandwidth and organizational commitment.

The Importance of Deep Dives: Data 360s

Data 360s can take anywhere from a couple of days to a couple of weeks. Sometimes you simply aren't able to capture the crucial data needed to test a hypothesis. In these cases, you need to develop new methods and invest time in collection.

The following are criteria for data 360:

1. Scale. The thing you're looking at needs to have a large enough impact to warrant the investment.
2. Buy-in. Are the people responsible for X, or those overseeing it, committed to implementing findings?
3. Significance. You're looking for unexplained success or underperformance. Why is thing X different?
4. Time. You must be able to provide the needed cross-departmental support to see the research through.

If you receive the same data question a third time, say no—and work on a solution that disengages the analyst from the process. If something is important enough to ask three times, it should likely be on demand for the end user. It requires that you give your data team time to invest in opening access—even if it means a short-term stagnation of insights while they build.

BUILDING A DATA TEAM

The first requirement included in all data job postings at DoSomething .org is a "strong sense of curiosity." We want people who are the smartest in the room, but not because they always know the answers—because they know how to ask the right questions. A core element of all data job descriptions is data exploration. This means anything from spending an hour reading through customer service logs or taking a day to build a model to see how interest in soup kitchens fluctuates throughout the year.

The data team's job is to analyze large and fast-moving data sets, detect changes in our members' behaviors, and test new products and ideas. Successful candidates will possess strong analytical skills and a steadfast sense of curiosity. Invest in people. Use open source when possible. Train staff. Above all, look for curiosity.

Scaling Impact: Knowing When and How to Use Outside Research

Being truly data-informed means knowing when to look externally to fill in the gaps that internal data and research cannot. You won't be able to use your employees for everything; many needs are more efficiently answered by preexisting, external sources. It is tempting to assume that all aspects of your business are so novel and earth shattering that no external commentator could possibly shed light on your pressing concerns. Of course, this is almost entirely wrong. Everything "new" has an extant corollary—whether you are launching a new flavor of potato chips, a revelatory weather app, or a new peer-to-peer bullying education program. Somewhere, someone smarter has invested considerable time answering your question (or something very close). An XYZ organization knows that it's acceptable—and advisable—to piggyback on the work of others. Why do something someone else has already done?

In the past, DoSomething.org has launched twenty-five campaigns each year across varying cause spaces. Moving forward, we are running two hundred annual campaigns, focusing on the more niche volunteer opportunities. This requires evidence that the outputs we will be measuring for each campaign correspond to the outcomes we desire. That is to say, we need to know that the actions we are asking our members to take (e.g., recycle fifty cans, hold a workshop on financial education) lead to the outcome that we want (e.g., reduce energy consumption, better financial planning).

DoSomething.org does not have the bandwidth or desire to attempt two hundred impact evaluations each year (and really, who would?). Any organization looking to diversify or scale up their programming or to expand their products and services must first shift from ex post facto evaluation and studies to evidence-based assumptions prior to launch. This requires that you look beyond an organization's own data and research teams to external research, partner organizations, or competitor comparisons.

Being data-informed in this sense means being astute consumers of research, knowing the difference between eureka! moments and dressed up bullshit. It also rewards inter-organizational connectivity.

QUESTIONS TO GET YOU STARTED:

1. If you could measure only one thing to gauge the success of your organization, what would it be?

2. Now pose this question to an assortment of colleagues from different departments. How do their answers differ? Do any overlap? If so, these spots of overlap are a great space from which to draw initial metrics.

3. Does senior management care what the data say? If the most highly paid members aren't pushing data-informed decision making, then no amount of grassroots data evangelism is going to revolutionize your organization. Convince the head first, and the body will eventually follow.

4. Once you have senior management on board, take a look at your organizational chart and identify the high-high, high-low, low-high, and low-low employees. Find the low-highs and see what you can do to help them. They will be your biggest allies as you push forward a data-informed culture.

5. What outcomes do you want to measure but are struggling to figure out how? Brand perception? Cause awareness? Peer-to-peer product promotion? Now try to come up with outputs that can reliably (and cheaply) measure them and that correlate with these outcomes. Most often those costly and impossible data points that you struggle with can be approximated by focusing on outputs better within your sight lines.

6. Are you asking questions in the right way?

7. Do you have analytics and reporting software that is collecting dust? If so, then you are probably overspending on technology at the expense of analysts. Remember: always spend more on staffing than tools.

8. Can everyone on staff tell you how the organization is performing? Would they even consider success the same way? You must provide a common framework for defining organizational success.

9. Have you ever ignored a data-informed recommendation? Why? Did you think the data was wrong or incomplete? Or did it simply not conform with long-standing institutional knowledge?

10. Do your qualitative and quantitative analysts work together? Do insights flow back and forth? Do you see the two as part of the process?

11. Are your organizational metrics encouraging the behavior you anticipated? Are employees chasing numbers, or are they contributing to the greater good?

ABOUT THE CONTRIBUTOR

Jeff Bladt is the chief data officer at DoSomething.org. He directs quantitative and qualitative research, and evangelizes for data-informed decision making. Each year he oversees the National Survey on Young People and Volunteering and has done targeted research into youth perceptions of bullying and gun policy. Jeff has an AB and MPP from the University of Chicago, where he studied economics and public policy. He has presented on data strategy at places including New York University, Harvard Graduate School of Education, and the Ad Council, and has published in the *Chicago Policy Review* and *Harvard Business Review*. He also likes sandwiches.

FIVE

BRAND

• • •

HOW YOUR IDENTITY INFLUENCES EVERYTHING

Farah Sheikh, Former Campaigns Manager: Education

W hat is a brand? Is it a logo? Is it a person? Is it a product? An idea? In truth, a brand is all of those things . . . and more. It's the way people answer the telephone. It's the quality of toilet paper the company stocks in the office bathroom. It's the way we interact with our mailman. It's the office address. It's the font on our website. It's everything we do, both intended and unintended.

DEFINING YOUR BRAND

Our brand is reflected in every single initiative we pursue. Internally, our brand provides employee identity, drives our decision-making process, attracts and retains talent, and is pervasive in the office we all call home. Externally, a strong brand guides the partners with whom we work, provides strategic direction in the communications and products we build, and inspires a level of recognition and engagement. A strong brand makes it easier to attract new employees and to find funding or strategic partners.

The DoSomething.org brand provides a filter through which we make every organizational decision. It gives us a sense of flexibility— one that makes working with a brand like AARP a no-brainer—along the strict principles to never, ever, say yes to a tobacco company who wants us to run their Corporate Social Responsibility (CSR) program. Our brand provides the guidelines we use to decide whether or not to run a campaign. "Does this feel like 'us'?" is one of the most common questions asked during a campaign brainstorm. And we all know exactly what that question means. Does this fit our brand? Would we feel proud to put this into the world with the DoSomething.org name attached to it? If the answer is no, then we don't run it.

Simple, youthful, and purposeful are DoSomething.org's brand guidelines and the three qualities that steer us in working with our audience. They empower us to give young people the tools they need to make a real, measurable impact in their communities. It allows us to make decisions that are best not only for us, but for them. And it makes sure that we hire people we actually like.

We work with some of the biggest brands in the world, and we want to work with even more; however, we will never compromise our integrity or our users' trust. Our website, pitch materials, and partnership proposals all sing true to our brand by using our colors, our language, and our personality. No potential corporate or strategic partner will ever be surprised to hear that we never require money, a car, or an old person (over 26) to participate in our campaigns. No Fortune 500 company will ever be able to twist our arm for us to sell them our mobile list.

Once your organization is clear about its brand, it becomes your guiding principle. You can then have confidence in the decisions you make based on this definition of who you are—not for money or press. Authenticity is essential in the branding game.

Tweetable Takeaway

Decide on your brand guidelines and stick with them—don't waver because you think you can make something (or someone) fit.

HOW YOUR BRAND GUIDES DECISIONS

We build products that meet our audience's volunteering needs. A few years ago, we pivoted to primarily using SMS (text) communications with our members because we weren't getting enough of a response on e-mail. We focus our efforts on products that make volunteering easier and more fun for our users. Beyond that, our pride in our brand translates to pushing out products that we believe in, that we're proud of, and that we think are beautiful. We never ship ugly. We'll explore how to establish your brand and how to use it to guide your decisions later in this chapter.

Any cause, anytime, anywhere. Our campaigns, our culture, our organization—we're big, we're loud, and we're easy (to understand, to join, and to advocate for).

YOUR VALUE SHOULD BE CLEAR, WITHOUT A "MISSION"

According to Charles Hill, author of *Strategic Management: An Integrated Approach*, a mission statement is a company's, organization's, or person's statement of purpose—the reason for existing. The mission should guide actions, spell out the overall goal, provide a path, and direct decision making.

Your company's reason for existence should be glaringly obvious in the work that you do. The energy our members feel around the campaigns we run and the causes we support doesn't come from a manifesto written on the wall; it comes from our brand. Most "mission statements" go unseen by the very audience for whom they are meant. Without searching online, I have no idea what the mission statements are for Nike or Coca-Cola or Facebook; I do, however, know what their brands are and what they stand for. I can think of three words that describe each of them immediately. And I know this because of the way their products translate meaning to me.

We don't have a mission statement at DoSomething.org. We have guiding principles and strategic goals. We have several reasons for existing, ranging from giving young people their first taste of volunteerism to shifting the public's perception of lazy teens.

Does your organization have a mission statement? Can you tell me verbatim what it is? Can your customers tell me what it is? Does it truly guide your decisions, your services, and your value to the customer, or does it remain pinned up on corkboards in conference rooms, yellowing with age?

HOW TO ENFORCE THE BRAND

Our guiding principles are painted around our office for all to see. "Fight for the User," a principle we use when making tech and user experience decisions, keeps us focused on our audience. This is especially helpful when figuring out the dynamics of our campaigns. Recently, we proposed a platform shift for a campaign called Fed Up that asked young people to paint a picture of the state of school lunches by uploading photos of theirs. In 2013, we ran the campaign on our website and measured the number of shares we received on lunch photos teens uploaded. The share numbers were low and very far from our goals; but the engagement numbers were through the roof. Teens were voting an average of eighty times per photo on whether they'd eat the posted lunch or toss it in the garbage. To increase the number of shares—and the campaign's virality—we proposed shifting the platform from our website to Tumblr, where shares are inherent and content is king, but voting doesn't exist. This proposal didn't pass—and it was a good reminder that we don't want to take the fun out of our campaigns and force our members to take an action they aren't interested in taking. Voting is what our members prefer—so we're sticking with that.

There are several ways your company can enforce its brand. Painting on the walls is one thing, but more feasible is ensuring that you have a fresh and up-to-date Communications Guide that all employees use for externally facing documents. It should include everything from the colors you use, the words you use to describe your target audience (for example, we use "young person" instead of "teen"), to your off-limits terms (we hate the word "pledge"). Maintaining and enforcing the brand is the job of our entire staff. Our entire team reviews the brand every year during our Staff Retreat. We do an exercise where we ask ourselves: If DoSomething.org died, what would be on its tombstone? Every person has a say. The process is enlightening and gets everyone reinvested in the organization. Even our new staff members are able to do a brand exercise during their onboarding process.

Tweetable Takeaway

Create and maintain a Communications Guide that houses guidelines for all external communications.

HOW DESIGN HAS AN IMPACT ON YOUR BRAND

Design is important to us from both a marketing and utilization perspective. Recently, we've begun to appreciate and focus on the importance of user experience design. It's an essential part of not just understanding our audience, but understanding what they want to do with us and determining how we can help them do it. As we continue to revive our website and improve our communications to become two-way instead of one-way, user experience design helps us build brand equity at multiple touch points.

For each campaign we run, we launch a separate "microsite" or a full-blown page within our greater DoSomething.org site. About two years ago, we started building our microsites mobile first, ensuring that they were responsive, looked beautiful, and worked well on a smartphone. We had learned that a large percentage of our members were accessing our site on their phone—and at the time, it looked terrible. So we shifted strategy to design for where our users were, instead of focusing on making the desktop model the best it could be.

We also know that our members are not patient online. They aren't going to dig for hours to find what they want, even if they know it's there somewhere. If they can't get what they want clearly and beautifully, they'll bounce. The "Fight for the User" message reminds us of our user-first mentality. We may want them to sign up first, but they won't do so until they have the information they're seeking. So we started watching what our members do when they interact with our site, and used that intel to make more informed decisions—simply by asking them what they want and building to their needs. We've tested and built a sign-up process that makes users happy first and us happy second. We're increasing interaction on our site, and decreasing the dev time it takes to build a good product.

We adhere to three tenets for web and graphic design: youthful, clean, and purposeful. Brand and design work together to create a feeling that people have when they think about your organization. Asking a random sample of ten teens will show you what people think DoSomething.org is: fun, young, excited. Take our logo out of the mix, and you still get those feelings from our microsite. Every design decision is strategic and purposeful. One year, I was working with our designer, Keri, trying to create a logo for our music education campaign, Band Together. It was one of the longest design processes we've undergone, and Nancy pushed us on every iteration to explain the purpose behind music notes or headphones. In the end, Keri created a beautiful logo and didn't even need to explain that the campaign was about music education; the branding made it clear.

Tweetable Takeaway
Don't arbitrarily choose colors and images; make sure that all visual aspects of your brand collateral are purposeful.

Previously, each of our campaigns had a totally new look and feel—different header, different logo, and different tonality. To be honest, it was a little crazy. Now we work off of a purposeful, youthful, and clean template for all of our campaigns. Unique tonality will come through in the photos and content we use, but we don't need to reinvent the wheel every time we build a campaign—and neither do you.

Tweetable Takeaway
Design consistency is your best friend. It creates recognition among your customers and makes for a stronger brand altogether.

My favorite recent brand story is from our Annual Meeting. There is a strong contingent of Beyoncé superfans in our office to the point that it has become part of our social culture. On any given day, someone will start blasting "Flawless" or do the "Drunk in Love" dance on their way out of a meeting. Our Annual Meeting is a time to celebrate our success with partners and pat ourselves on the back for the past year. Keri decided that the back of the program would say "WE WOKE UP LIKE THIS . . . FLAWLESS." It was one of the most tweeted, Instagrammed, and well-liked design decisions of the day. It was purposeful (because it reflected our brand), it was youthful (because it invoked Beyoncé), and it was clean. And it sent a message, loud and clear, about who we are and what's important to us.

THE FIVE COMPONENTS OF A STRONG BRAND

Nancy gives a presentation every year at our Staff Retreat about the five elements of a strong brand: simplicity, specificity, uniqueness, consistency, and relevancy. We use these to evaluate everything we do—every campaign we launch, every product we offer, every presentation and pitch we give.

Simplicity

Like most customers, our members embrace simplicity. Each of our campaigns must have one simple call to action that any teen can accomplish without money, a car, or an adult. Telling them to "hold an event in your school to raise money for this organization that saves the dolphins in the Caribbean" does not fit this bill. The Campaigns team regularly does an exercise where we have to pitch our campaign to the rest of the organization in one sentence. "Collect jars of peanut butter and donate to your local food pantry in the spring when donations are most needed" sounds a lot simpler than the dolphin fundraiser, no?

Specificity

Adding specificity to our campaigns is often what distinguishes them from the other volunteer opportunities our teens have. When we first started focusing on environmental impacts in schools, we ran a campaign called Green Your School that listed twenty-five different ways our members could make their school a more environmentally friendly place. It was a well-meaning campaign—but not one that many people participated in, likely because we didn't provide specific ideas about actions to take. Last year, Hilary, our Environment and Animals Campaign Specialist, decided to focus the campaign on one of the biggest energy sucks in school: vampire energy (a term that refers to the electric power consumed by electronic and electrical appliances while they are switched off or in a standby mode). We called it Don't Be A Sucker and asked young people to unplug appliances in their schools when they weren't being used. Because it was specific, it was much easier to measure impact.

Uniqueness

Being unique is a top priority for DoSomething.org. We run very differently than most nonprofits. For one thing, we never, ever ask our members for money. We provide a service and deliver concrete impact for the young people we serve. None of our campaigns have been done before by other organizations at our scale. For instance, our Give A Spit campaign asks teens to run drives in their communities to get people to join the National Bone Marrow Registry that services those suffering from blood cancer. Although other organizations participate in this kind of activity, none focus on the ease of registering. The majority of them use scary terminology and diagrams of what your marrow extraction looks like—and then they wonder why no one signs up! We focus on how easy it is to get registered, and how impactful your donation will be to someone in need. We aren't the experts on the science behind it, but we know that most of our teens believe that it's worth saving someone's life.

Consistency

Advocating for consistency may seem to challenge our innovative and adaptive tendencies; however, our members have come to expect a certain level of sameness in everything we do when it comes to brand. All our campaigns have a different call to action; each of them focuses on a different cause; and they all take place on a different platform. But every campaign gives young people an easy way to take action on a cause young people care about. The fundamentals of what we do don't change. We stand for something, and that's how we build brand loyalty.

Relevance

Relevance is the last but possibly the most important component of our brand. We've had potential partners tell us that they really want to work with us on a campaign around an issue that fits their brand. And of course, corporate partnership is great; it's what keeps our lights on, our doors open, and our impact real. But sometimes we have to say no to a potential partner who cares about a cause that isn't relevant to our teens. We don't try to compel our members to care about a cause they feel doesn't have an impact on them. We address causes and issues that are relevant to them—and we know they're relevant because we ask.

CREATING A STRONG INTERNAL CULTURE WITH NO MONEY

It's no coincidence that every employee in our office feels our culture is our identity. Creating and maintaining the DoSomething.org culture is a shared priority of the whole staff. When I describe the interview process to my friends, they scoff in disbelief—and then proclaim they wished they worked somewhere that placed such high value on the personalities of their staff members, instead of the contents of their résumés.

DoSomething.org has several components we believe contribute to making our culture so great. Adopting these components will help you define a strong culture your employees can believe in.

Transparency

Internal transparency about organizational goals and progress is one of the best ways to shape employee identity. When the staff convened in Utah for a three-day intensive workshop one spring, we realized that we were not delivering on a brand promise of giving young people a way to take action around any cause they care about at any time. We used those three days to figure out ways to address this, came up with a new strategy, and we knew what we needed to do to get there. Every person on staff knew their role in our restructuring; everyone was filled with an energy and excitement to get back to New York City and get started.

We wouldn't have felt that way without a widespread belief that our work contributes to an overall organizational goal. Our internal transparency begets a level of personal satisfaction tied to our organizational success. In short, I know exactly how what I'm doing contributes to overall goals. My job plays a significant part in our organization's ability to continue to innovate and reach teens where they are.

Hiring and Recruiting

Our culture is the reason talented people want to work for us and the reason that they stay once they start. Being the largest organization for young people and social change gives people a reason to want to be here. Growth opportunities and consistent innovation give employees a reason to stick around and take part in change. The DoSomething.org brand is our most effective recruiting tool and the reason we will probably never have to hire a recruiter. Our Tech team is the largest team in the organization, and it's not because we're revolutionizing the Internet. The culture of DoSomething.org is so unique to our brand that we attract some of the best developers in the nation because they want to feel good and excited about the work they do.

Nurturing Individuality

Understanding how to nurture your existing staff members so that your organization's true culture can emerge is even more crucial than hiring. You don't need a huge budget for "staff bonding" (or whatever your office calls its booze allotment). It simply requires that you acknowledge your staff members' qualities and your brand's priorities—and find a happy marriage between the two. Your culture development should focus on staff development, appreciation, and balance.

Our existing staff is full of strong personalities and diverse passions. We have a male model running our social media, a sex and relationships writer editing all of our content, a back-end developer is also the voice of our YouTube puppet, and a former film student is the head of our Campaigns team. That's only four of fifty. We love this about our staff. Instead of squashing outside passions or projects, we encourage and celebrate being involved in things that fulfill you.

Each year, we do a Secret Santa gift exchange. There's a (very low) dollar limit, and each person draws the name of someone else on staff. Then, on the happiest day of the DoSomething.org year, we sit around a big Christmas tree, and each person opens a gift and guesses who gifted it. Last year, Greg, TMI's Lead Strategist, recorded an album and donated all of the funds to Donors Choose music programs across the country. His secret Santa, Ravelle from our Content team, contacted the teachers from all of the schools he sent money to and had their students write thank-you letters and send pictures. She then compiled them into a scrapbook—and when Greg opened it, there wasn't a dry eye in the house.

Through outside passions, we also have a much clearer view of our internal resources. One year, for our music education campaign, we decided to create a crowdsourced music video on YouTube that encouraged teens to share their message of the importance of music education in their lives. We had six challenges that we released over the course of six weeks that made up different parts of the song. They range from "clap your hands to the beat" to "hold up a sign that says what music means to you." We received hundreds of submissions, and we'd promised that each teen who submitted a video would be included in the overall video. Dave, our Head of Campaigns and previous film student, was a huge asset in producing the video. He had a knowledge base and a passion that allowed us to create a product that felt impactful, fun, and badass.

Examples of using staff members' passions for development are in no short order around here. My biggest passion is food justice and access—and I was able to use it to run a campaign on food in schools and on how to empower young people to be part of the conversation. A staff member who considered going to graduate school for international development was given the reins to expand our international affiliates program, and has grown it to eight countries in a little over a year. We understand our employees and love when they use what they love to continue to mold our culture.

> ## Tweetable Takeaway
> An XYZ company's staff is its greatest cultural asset. Nurture individual, personal goals in order to get the best work out of them.

Appreciation

Organizations commonly show appreciation through raises, promotions, and bonuses. We have those—in addition to a whole lot of other ways. Though raises may make your morning coffee a bit easier on the bank, they don't make you want to come to work in the morning. Using your culture to cultivate effective practices that are true to your brand and the organization's energy create much more meaningful shows of appreciation than an extra bump in the bank.

Chapter Two discussed our Wednesday Staff Meeting, where each person shares one accomplishment from the past week, one goal for the next week, and one request they have from the staff. We use the aforementioned Penguin as a badge of honor and a way for someone else on staff to give you a giant pat on the back for a job well done. And it doesn't cost a thing.

However, we don't limit expression of appreciation to internal meetings and traditions. As mentioned earlier, a feeling of collective accountability for organizational success lends itself to widespread external celebration of internal wins. We frequently celebrate organizational wins as well as individual wins on our personal social media channels. The employees at DoSomething.org feel a sense of pride when their coworkers achieve greatness.

In 2013, our CMO Naomi was selected as a PR Person to Watch by PR News Online. The outpouring of love and support I saw on my coworkers' Facebook and Twitter accounts was unbelievable. People were so proud to be working with someone like Naomi, who is not only strategic and driven, but also a pleasure to work with.

The DoSomething.org social media account is used to celebrate our culture and employees. Nancy posts frequently about an amazing thing our data scientists are doing over the weekend or tweets at a cute employee of a friendly organization about all the single girls at the office. It's strategic, but it also invokes a sense of pride.

Employees share our favorite member stories: Campaigns reports back photos and moments of pride with one another. Our jobs are a huge part of our lives, and not because we spend a lot of time here—it's because of the brand. Each person here is driven by social change, inspired by young people, and excited to show our appreciation for our awesome jobs both internally and externally.

Work–Life Balance—for Real

The final focus for cultivating DoSomething.org's culture has been a sense of balance. There is a laundry list of traditions and best practices to which we adhere in order to ensure that employees are leading healthy lives and have the ability to balance work and personal life (even if these things start to blend).

When I first started at DoSomething.org, we were going through a website flip that required an insane amount of dev time and long hours by our engineers. One day, Nancy announced that she needed a conference room for the full day because a masseuse was coming in to give the whole Tech team massages. Imagine how wonderful that felt after hours of leaning over a computer trying to make sure the entire website for a Web-based platform wasn't going down.

After two years of employment at DoSomething.org, employees are given the opportunity to take a sabbatical for a month during which they volunteer at another organization anywhere in the world. This opportunity is beneficial for the employee, who gets a new experience, most often in a foreign country, but also for the organization, which gets to benefit from the renewed energy and excitement of employees who elect to take sabbatical. Balancing the experience you have at DoSomething .org with a close view of how another organization works is unique and indescribably effective.

Tweetable Takeaway

Overworking your employees will lead to fatigue and resentment. Encourage them to have a life outside of work so that they return refreshed and excited.

EMPLOYEES AS BRAND AMBASSADORS: HIRING ROCK STARS AND MAKING THEM ADVOCATES

Our hiring process is unique, and some might say intense. We like to call it effective and comprehensive—and we take it very seriously.

Know Your Criteria

Our most important criterion for hiring is culture fit. Your résumé, cover letter, and writing sample will show us what we need to know about your experience. But we also want to know the weirdest thing about you and the most recent concert you attended. My favorite interview questions include:

1. If you could be a food, what would you be and why?
2. If you had to replace your arm with anything, what would it be and why?
3. If you could have any superpower, what would it be?
4. When was the last time you danced alone in your room?
5. What is your go-to karaoke song?

Our interview process allows us to protect our culture, and in turn, our brand. Any candidate who applies for a job with DoSomething.org will always remember his or her interview. It's big (every staff member is invited to participate in the final interview), and it's loud (no one is shy about asking the hard-hitting karaoke questions). It may not be easy for the candidate, but it's easy for us to make a decision afterward.

> **Tweetable Takeaway**
> XYZers involve multiple staff in the hiring of new team members to serve as a culture check.

Before you start interviewing for a position, ask yourself and your staff to name the most important characteristics for keeping your culture alive. What are the three questions that will show you whether or not someone is the right fit? Then you always have those to use as a gut check.

We hire for passion, and not just passion for our brand. You can teach someone how to be a good project manager or how to do effective research. You can't teach someone how to care wholeheartedly about something; that quality is inherent. It drives you to work hard and not quit until you've done your absolute best. It's what makes other people want to work with you, whether it's members, customers, coworkers, or strategic partners. It translates to interesting people, diverse culture, and great work.

Most people who come to work at DoSomething.org are already passionate about youth, social change, or any combination of the two. But most still undergo a pretty significant transformation during their first few weeks of working here. You go from being a fan of the organization to a full-fledged advocate.

There are a number of ways our brand and culture inspire this transformation—we boil them down to sharing wins, giving permission to be loud, and creating internal and external opportunities for growth.

Celebrate Wins

It is a priority with every campaign we run to give our members a reason to feel like they were part of something bigger and achieved a level of success. Whether it's a thank-you package full of craft supplies, candy, and a note to the top hundred card makers for our Birthday Mail campaign, or an e-mail to every participant announcing with great fanfare that they played a role in helping to collect over a million pairs of jeans for Teens for Jeans, we always say thank you.

When we reached one million mobile members, we found the young lady who had been the millionth person to sign up via SMS for our campaigns and surprised her and her best friend at their local pizza parlor. We brought a huge cake, balloons, a video camera, and a trip for her and her family to Disney World. She had no idea she had done anything special, but we considered her an essential part of our celebration and we wanted to share that with her.

Whenever we launch a new campaign, the campaign lead gives an internal presentation about the issue we're addressing, the call to action, and the impact we're hoping for. This all kicks off with the gong we first discussed in Chapter One. Launching a campaign is hard work, and we love celebrating it.

Nancy has a habit of buying a bright orange bottle of Veuve Clicquot for people who go above and beyond their day-to-day jobs. She gives it as a personal and genuine thank-you for kicking ass. It's not showy, and it's not public, but it makes the person feel damn good for the win. Not

many companies can point to an example that shows its employees how much their work means personally to the CEO.

Permission to be loud is better expressed as "encouragement to be as loud as possible." DoSomething.org encourages employees to be vocal. We are not an organization led by the whims of one person or group of people. We thrive on conversation, challenge, and creative thinking.

Innovate Regularly

Each week, on Wednesday mornings, we have our Innovation Meeting. The entire staff all crams into one room and listens to presentations about changes to process, product, or ideas. The presentations are rooted in data or intuition and propose a change to the way we do things. It's crucial for us to hold these meetings weekly because we are constantly evaluating our brand, communications, and process. Every person is encouraged to bring up ideas or questions. These meetings are some of the most stimulating conversation to happen all week. Several of our largest brand decisions have been made in those meetings.

When we launch a campaign, we have a meeting during its second week to analyze how we are pacing and what we can do to pivot our strategy to optimize growth. The Data team, the Campaign lead, and Marketing team sit in a room and talk about how to make the campaign better, stronger, and louder. We don't want to just see what happens after eight weeks and then analyze it when everything's over and it's too late to improve anything. Updating strategy happens early, and in a big way.

And campaign ideas don't just come from the Campaigns team.

DoSomething.org has an open, creative process that facilitates idea creation from every corner of the organization. Some of my favorite campaign ideas have come from Jeff, our Chief Data Officer. This not only helps keep all teams invested in the campaigns, but also ensures that we're presenting and running a diverse set of campaigns that interest a wider variety of people.

> ### Tweetable Takeaway
> Let all staff contribute to the goals of your org. Let people work outside their prescribed roles—you'll be surprised what happens.

Give Growth Opportunities

When you first start at DoSomething.org, Nancy sits with you in a room and tells you that we expect you to do two things: (1) hit a home run in the first three months you're here, and (2) do something amazing in the next four or five years, whether it's here or somewhere else. These expectations lend themselves to an organization that is ripe with internal and external growth opportunities.

Our C-level employees are invited to speak at hundreds of conferences a year. Although they could never actually attend every conference at the same time they're running an organization, the real reason they don't go to everything is because they believe in giving staff members some of these opportunities to speak about DoSomething.org. Encouraging a Tech team member to speak at a conference on innovation in the nonprofit world gives the employee a unique experience and presents DoSomething.org as a well-rounded organization. We can offer different perspectives according to what the conference is about and speak on a genuine level as an employee who has accountability for the work we do.

Our COO, Aria, recently passed on a conference to me to which other organizations are sending their COO's and executive directors—not because she doesn't think it's important, but because the conference focuses on working at a summer camp with youth, something I have experience with and passion for. Her generosity gives me a chance to get exposure and public speaking experience, and also allows for us to give a tailored, specific message as an organization.

DoSomething.org's brand is all about giving every teen an opportunity to take a volunteer action. They don't need to be the president of their student government, or have $1,000 to start their project. The same way our brand encourages growth and involvement from every person, our culture gives everyone from the Finance team to the Design team an opportunity to try something new. Our former finance and HR manager, Chaquana, and our TMI agency strategy associate attended a leadership conference together in Disneyland. It might seem like a strange pairing, but everyone at DoSomething.org deserves a chance to try something new.

> ## Tweetable Takeaway
> Pizza with honey. Sriracha and chocolate. Unexpected combos sometimes yield AMAZING results!

Our organization encourages outside development as well. I don't think there is one person on staff who doesn't have an outside passion and commitment. Naomi, our CMO, plays on a soccer team. I write for a travel startup. Ben, our content writer, also had a writing gig with *Glamour* magazine. As an organization that values innovation and diverse opinions, external opportunities for growth come in a variety of forms.

> ## Tweetable Takeaway
> Encourage employees to grow on their own and pursue passions. This will lead to more well-rounded employees for you.

INTERNAL CULTURE AS EXTERNAL BRAND

It's always funny to me when prospective employees ask me to describe DoSomething.org's culture. I oblige, but I also usually urge them to do their research. There are no surprises. The DoSomething.org that you see on our Facebook page, in our campaigns, on our Instagram, and on our home page is the DoSomething.org that I go to work at every day. Our culture is our brand.

There is a sense of pride that comes with working at an organization like ours—one that's obvious to everyone who comes into contact with our brand. Whenever I talk to my friends about my job, the reaction is consistently "DoSomething.org seems like such a great place to work." And it is. There is no hiding the pride we all feel in the campaigns we execute, the teens on whom we have an impact and who have an impact on us, and the internal celebration of our staff.

Every campaign that we run paints a clear picture of our culture. When we were first strategizing for the Pregnancy Text, there was so much internal back-and-forth about the best way to approach an emotionally charged issue like teen pregnancy. We've seen so many brands and organizations crash and burn by pandering safe sex and abstinence to teens. The majority of campaigns are incredibly condescending or terrifying— and neither is effective. There is nothing interesting or helpful about treating young people like they are idiots.

We have a phrase at DoSomething.org that we used as guidance during Pregnancy Text: "Never take away their tater tots." In other words, we are not the organization to tell young people what not to do; there are enough people doing that already. Our members are on our level—they are smart as hell and savvier than they're given credit for. They don't respond to lectures, but they're influenced by friends.

We therefore decided to explore how having a child would affect a teen's life that day, not fifteen years in the future. Teens don't particularly care about what their income disparity will be in comparison to someone who doesn't have a kid. We used their phones, because that's how they talk to their friends. And we were funny, not dark and dooming. In Pregnancy Text, you can practically hear the voice of our Content team and Alyssa, the campaign lead. The baby in your phone is witty, smart, and sassy. It makes you think twice without telling you your life is going to end, and it allows young people to be the ones starting the conversation.

Thumb Wars, our anti–texting and driving campaign, is another great example of our culture affecting our external brand. Research shows us that scare tactics don't work in distracted driving campaigns. There is a sense of foreboding and maybe an uneasiness that comes with seeing a smashed-up car outside your high school, but when you are behind the wheel, it feels like it could happen to anyone else but you.

We took the superhero approach with Thumb Wars because, well, we love superheroes. Who doesn't? The best ones are regular people who found out they have a gift and a calling to help save the world. We believe that every teen who takes action through one of our campaigns is a superhero in his or her own right. Our five conference rooms are named after superhero lairs, my personal favorite being Wonder Woman's Themyscira. We believe that teens have the superpowers necessary to help save their friends from the dangers of texting and driving. Instead of lecturing or scaring them, we give them thumb socks to share with their friends who text and drive to serve as a reminder to keep your thumbs (and the rest of your hands) on the wheel.

Thumb Wars and Pregnancy Text are two of our most successful campaigns because they are the truest to our brand. They're the most often spoken about at conferences and mentioned as favorites by partners and applicants. We find that when we strike a balance between brand, impact, and accessibility, our campaigns return the type of results that have us popping bottles of champagne (or at least eating Oreos in celebration).

Our teens are our greatest extension of our internal brand. We consider our brand advocates to be our most valuable asset—and those are the teens on the ground running our campaigns and telling their friends about how we helped them launch their project. Without young people, we would just be a cause marketing shop. It is the teen who runs his first Teens for Jeans drive and collects five hundred pairs from his church youth group who provides us the most pride. The young person who creates over a thousand birthday cards to send to a shelter for a kid who might not have a birthday party this year is the DoSomething.org representative we love. The teen who gets a call to save a five-year-old girl's life because she swabbed her cheek during Give A Spit and is a match, and doesn't hesitate to say yes, is a hero to us. These teens are our brand, our culture, and our reason for existing.

The same way we celebrate our members and their impact, we celebrate staff and the hard work that happens in-house. As fun and vibrant as our culture is, I have never been surrounded by as many hard working people as I am when I walk in the door at 9 A.M.

Our internal faming of a developer who hacks a platform and makes it easier for our members to sign up for campaigns, or a designer who creates smart, clean, youthful work, will become fodder for DoSomething.org's Twitter feed. We can't stop talking about the things that we're proud of, and it encourages our members to be open and excited to share their wins with us even more. Just as we value staffers who go above and beyond, we love our members who do the same.

That being said, we also know that our audience, like so many others, is fickle. They change their minds as much as they change their shirts. One day, Facebook is the way to go, and the next second it's all about Snapchat. I see that reflected in our strategy as an organization.

Three years ago, we were trying to e-mail a few scholarship winners and weren't hearing back from them. We had reached out several times to no avail. Mike Fantini, who is now our head of Product, had the idea to text them. We had their phone numbers, so why not? We heard back from all of them within minutes. This revelation created a huge shift for us. We won a grant to shift our communication strategy to SMS and now have over two million mobile members in our database. We don't wait to become experts in something that teens are using—we change and adapt our strategy to stay relevant to them. We don't push them to communicate with us on a platform they aren't using (e-mail); it's our job to meet them where they are (via text messages). We don't just emphasize innovation and transparency. It's also about being true to your brand through every outlet that may not be changing.

> **Tweetable Takeaway**
> Establish norms that speak to what you value and how you function, regardless of platform.

Our job titles are another way we express our brand. CEO Nancy's title is "Chief Old Person." Even though she is no longer the oldest person in the organization, it establishes the norm that we don't hire people who are out of touch or too far from our audience. Our hiring manager goes by "Head of Fun." She's responsible for maintaining the majority of our office culture. From making sure that we always have hot chocolate and marshmallows in the winter to planning our staff retreat every summer and managing every new applicant, she is literally the keeper of fun at DoSomething.org.

We don't hesitate to create an opportunity where none previously existed if it fits with our brand and culture. Bryce, whom I mentioned earlier, is on our Content team in a position that didn't exist a year ago. He came to us as an intern in the summer of 2013 and was one of the most vibrant, passionate interns we've ever had. He brought energy to the organization that we didn't have and realized we loved. So, we made a position for him, because he served the dual purpose of fitting in while shaking things up. In the month that he's been an official employee, he's taken over our Instagram feed, established our presence on Snapchat, and added a healthy dose of different dance moves to our afternoon dance breaks.

Your organization's brand is the number one identifying factor both inside and outside its four walls. Ensuring a strong brand that pervades everything you do will not only increase employee buy-in, but also customer loyalty. Being consistent and true to the brand you establish will have greater benefits than paying some agency for a fancy "rebrand." Spoiler alert: it won't work. Instead, put effort and energy into your own brand ideals and the way they translate internally and externally.

QUESTIONS TO GET YOU STARTED:

1. What does your internal culture say about your external brand? Do they match?

2. Does your mission statement inspire your employees or hang forgotten on the wall?

3. What five adjectives would you use to describe your brand? Would your audience use the same ones?

4. Is your voice in external communications consistent?

5. Do you count your employees as some of your best brand advocates?

6. Are your employees proud to share your content on their social networks?

7. Do you know your employees' individual passions? Do you encourage them to pursue them?

8. What is your value to the audience?

ABOUT THE CONTRIBUTOR

Farah Sheikh recently left DoSomething.org, where she was education campaigns manager, to be a Producer at Big Spaceship. At DoSomething.org, she performed research about the education space, developed insights on what young people want to change and how they want to take action, and built and executed strategies for education cause campaigns. Prior to arriving at DoSomething.org, Farah worked at Ogilvy Entertainment in branded content.

She's passionate about food, travel, new people, and the intersection of those three things.

SIX

BUSINESS DEVELOPMENT

• • •

HOW TO FORM MEANINGFUL RELATIONSHIPS

Muneer Panjwani, Business Development Manager and Liz Eddy, Special Project Manager

Asking someone to move in with you upon first meeting is not a good idea. Neither is asking someone you've just met to fund your new program. Both give you a really low chance of success, and a really high chance of looking like a creep. And, of course, you don't want to be a creep. You want to be a friend, a confidant, an adviser. Think about the classic car salesmen—pushy, über competitive, and kind of annoying. They care far more about making the sale than about anything that you, the buyer, are getting out of it.

The most important word in fundraising isn't money; it's relationship. Research continues to prove that the happiest people have one thing in common—strong relationships. And the same holds true for successful organizations. Their leaders often have strong, long-term relationships with influencers across many industries.

For a company to succeed, it needs partners that believe in it and want to be part of its long-term vision. It takes one-quarter of the effort to maintain an existing partner than to find a new one, so why not start each relationship with the goal of building a long-term partnership? It's a rookie mistake to view people who work at big companies or foundations as ATMs with legs. They're people first, and people like to feel connected and valued.

IDENTIFYING THE RIGHT PARTNERS

We're allergic to the word sponsor; it makes us vomit contracts and receipts. Sponsor puts money as the central, most important part of a relationship. It also creates a hierarchy of power between the one giving the money and the one receiving it. Relationships are built on a foundation of shared values and goals between two equal partners.

The word "partner" inherently states that each party has something valuable to offer to reach the mutual goals of a partnership. It's about symbiosis, not cannibalism. One may have money, the other expertise. One may have a distribution network, the other a unique service. Strong relationships and successful partnerships require each partner to recognize and advocate for the unique assets they bring to the table. This section will detail some key points to think about to identify a partner that is right for you.

Look for Partners with Shared Values

Finding the perfect partner is a value play. Money is of course important, but it shouldn't force you to change your values. We at DoSomething.org always ask three important questions when looking for a partner.

1. Does the company want to create change around something our audience cares about?
2. Are they a brand fit for DoSomething.org?
3. Will working with them make our staff cry?

These are our nonnegotiables. We care about what young people care about, not what the CEO of a company cares about—and the first question makes sure we hold true to that. The second ensures that our partners understand that DoSomething.org has a unique voice and approach to social change. They need to buy into that in order to partner with us. The third is just to make it clear that we don't work with jerks. Nancy has publicly stated that if any partner makes our staff cry, we won't work with them again. These parameters help us keep good partners around and weed out the not-so-great ones. Of course, partnerships are more than these three things; but it's imperative to establish your own nonnegotiables before diving into a long-term relationship with the wrong partner.

Tweetable Takeaway

Ask staff to identify necessary partner values. Use these as parameters to make sure future partners are a solid fit.

Look for Partners Your Mom Would Approve Of

Not everyone you date gets to meet your mom or dad, because not everyone is worthy. The same approach can work for evaluating professional partners. Your partners should make you proud, and you should be excited to introduce them to your staff, your board, on stage at a conference, and even to your other partners.

Before you sign on the dotted line, ask yourself how this partnership will affect every aspect of the organization and the people who make it work. Look beyond someone's offering and ask:

1. Who will manage the day-to-day business of the partnership?
2. Will they micromanage your program, or do they trust you to do what you're good at?
3. Do they have other assets that could help the program succeed? Do you see deeper opportunities with them in the future?
4. Would you be comfortable having difficult conversations with them?

Partners are an extension of your brand, your network, and your staff. Make sure they're worthy of fulfilling that role. If getting on the phone with them evokes dread and anxiety, they're probably not the right partner.

Look for Partners Relevant to Your Target Audience

It goes without saying that your partners should care about whom you care about. DoSomething.org's member base is composed of thirteen- to twenty-five-year-olds, so all of our partners either serve that same audience or are looking to. If a partner ever asks us to expand our reach into another demographic, we simply answer no. In an effort to avoid even having to answer that question, our Business Development team does thorough research on potential partners' marketing goals and target audiences.

Find partners with common interests and goals, not partners who require you to change in order to fulfill their needs. If you struggle to find common goals, you'll likely be forced to change who you serve and how you work in order to make the partnership work. Very few things are worth changing your purpose.

Look for the Right Type of Funding

There are two types of funding: restricted and unrestricted. Restricted funding is money earmarked for a specific program, thus all money received must be spent on that program alone. Unrestricted funding is donated to support a specific program but does not need to be spent solely on that program. Both come with their share of pros and cons.

A no-strings-attached relationship with a funder is the dream. Money that isn't designated for a specific program allows organizations to innovate new ways to further their purpose, invest in new technology, and hire better staff. This is why DoSomething.org is over 80 percent corporate funded. The money we've raised from corporate partners has allowed us to become the experts on young people and social change, which in turn makes us more attractive to other corporate partners.

Restricted funding often comes from foundations and government agencies. This money comes with a lot of limitations, such as the percentage you can spend on staff and overhead. This can be frustrating because its staff working in offices with lights, computers, and phones that make each program happen.

This doesn't mean that corporate partners are the dream and foundations are a nightmare. Foundations often require extra work, but are more likely to give money to support a new idea than corporations are. When DoSomething.org began using SMS as a key member acquisition tool, we received funding (and a lot of trust) from the Omidyar Network, Knight Foundation, and Google Foundation that helped us increase our impact and our self-sustainability.

Foundation priorities are very different from those of a corporate partner. Foundations generally aren't looking for logo placement, millions of media impressions, or a celebrity spokesperson. They are looking for data and proof of impact, usually in the form of a mid-year or final report, or both. They are measuring their investments against other investments to prove the validity of their allocations. Their focus is impact.

Tweetable Takeaway

If you're looking for funding for a new idea, look to foundations first.

Donations from corporate partners are usually unrestricted. And though corporate partners have strings, they're a lot more flexible. This money usually comes from marketing or community engagement departments that want to "hire" a not-for-profit to fulfill their Corporate Social Responsibility (CSR) requirements. In return for partnering for an event or campaign, they want the organization to let their audience (and the world) know that they care about making a meaningful impact in the communities in which their customers and employees live. They're not as concerned about the breakdown of how their donation is spent as long as the organization is achieving mutually agreed-on goals and spending money responsibly. Like foundations, they care about impact, but place more emphasis on gathering data on participant numbers and media impressions, because those things affect their brand awareness and loyalty.

Think thoroughly about what type of funding is most valuable to your organization. DoSomething.org's massive reach in the thirteen- to twenty-five-year-old demographic makes it attractive to corporate partners who want access to our reach, expertise, and brand recognition. In return, we get the flexibility of spending what we need in order to keep the lights on and continue innovating. Our audience is constantly changing, and flexible spending allows us to test new ideas and hire the data geeks and programmers we need in order to keep up.

To convince a partner to give you unrestricted funding, you have to show them the value of your partnership—not the cost of your program. The difference is less about money and more about the level of expertise, impact, and exposure your partner will get by working with you. The actual cost of a program may be $10,000, but the value of working with you extends to the capability you bring to the table, the marketing partners you are able to engage at no cost to the partner, and your audience that trusts you. These are value-adds that a partner gets in addition to supporting that specific program. In addition, demonstrating the full scope of your work makes a more impressive and convincing pitch than showing them just the details of a particular program.

Tweetable Takeaway

Identify what you can offer that is attractive to a for-profit partner. Examine your reach, expertise, and relationships.

One source of funding isn't necessarily better than the other; it simply depends on what you're looking for. It's a good idea to diversify your funding so that you can continue to sustain your current programs AND innovate.

COMMUNICATION

Partnerships are typically agreements between two companies, but they're managed by people. Learn how to humanize your connections to yield better results.

Call Me, Maybe?

Do you know why telemarketers and sales e-mails are so bad at successfully selling you things? It's because all they do is talk about their company, their product, and how they will make your life/job/love life better. They focus the entire conversation on their values instead of your needs. These "pitches" are often based on an assumption they've made about what you need based on little to no research. It's annoying enough to have to hang up the phone or filter these e-mails out of your inbox; but it's especially uncomfortable when this happens in person. I often see well-meaning, passionate business development people approach leaders from different companies only to waste that opportunity talking about themselves.

Organizations seeking funding can get pretty "thirsty" in a room full of potential funders. It's easy to launch into pitch mode when you're sitting across from a marketing executive and all you see are dollar signs. It's much wiser to use that opportunity to ask questions about the company and get to know the people representing it. Then, when you e-mail them afterward, you have a specific interest of THEIRS to highlight and build off. You can learn that they spearheaded a unique program at their company or that they love running marathons or that their son just started second grade. These details will inform your ideas beyond just your own understanding of their priorities and goals and allow you to open with conversation, not an open hand. You'll have a much better chance of landing that first date (an official pitch meeting) this way than by touting your most recent quarterly dashboard numbers.

Tweetable Takeaway

Use initial face time with a potential partner to learn instead of pitch. Uncover three personal facts about the person.

It's totally OK to talk about your work and success, but you should find the best way to talk about it organically to avoid coming off "pitchy." If you give your ear to the other people, they'll give theirs in return. Corporate folks are tired of being pitched to at every turn; shifting the power dynamic is a welcome surprise that'll not only ensure that they remember you but also will provide a stronger foundation on which to build your relationship. People love talking about themselves. See funders as people, ask the right questions, and their answers might just be exactly what you needed to know to close the deal.

It's easy to fall into the pitch trap when it seems like you only have a few seconds to make your case before the other person rejects you like a judge on *America's Got Talent*. Let your work speak for itself with a story you share. The times I've bonded over someone's love for Alexander McQueen, Beyoncé, mutual contacts, or immigration rights are the times that I've created the strongest connections.

Following Up

A new employee at DoSomething.org gave me a business card of someone he met at dinner who he thought would be a great partner for us. I gave the card back to him and said he should follow up and introduce me. He said, "Sounds good; I'll do it next week." He was a recent college graduate, so I used that as a teaching moment for him: follow up immediately after you meet someone. You don't want to lose the momentum you're building by waiting even a few days. There are three different types of follow-ups that I've found to be successful:

1. Let's chat! I use this when I had a great conversation with someone who showed genuine interest in what DoSomething.org does. I may not have had enough time to tell more about DoSomething .org (because I was learning more about the person instead); or she may not have had time to go into more detail about what her company is doing (because we were busy bonding over Ryan Gosling). This is a great way to quickly follow up to say how you'd

love to learn more about her work (and perhaps mention how you watched *The Notebook* for the ninety-eighth time last night).

2. Here's more info! This works well when someone showed interest in a specific program I brought up during our conversation. It may or may not have been a DoSomething.org program, but helping to expand the person's knowledge on something he showed interest in shows that you listened and cared enough to follow up on it. Since we spent our time talking broadly about our work and how terrible that last panel was, this is an opportunity to guide the relationship to learn more about each other's work within a specific context. You can also use this tactic to introduce the person to one of your contacts, offer some resources that could help his programs or projects, or cite any supplementary materials that expand your in-person conversation.

3. Tell me more! When the other person brings up a successful program of hers in our conversation that I want to learn more about, I take this approach. It's yet another opportunity for her to talk more about her company's work so that you can evaluate if it's a good fit for your organization.

The goal in following up is twofold: (1) to build on the connection you made in person, and (2) to begin to find areas of potential partnership. You should know after one or two calls whether there is a possibility for a partnership—but even if there isn't, do not lose touch.

Stay in Touch

A passive contact today can be your biggest active partner in the future. If you've connected with someone but now is not the right time for a partnership, don't make the mistake of forgetting he exists.

Just letting the person know he's at top of mind for you will make you top of mind for him. Send regular e-mails to "check in" to see what's new in his life, and share a sentence or two about yours. Send him your quarterly dashboard, information about a recent award your company won, or a note of congrats for a recognition their company received. Invite him to your office parties and other events you might need a business date for. One of you may move to a different job, or company priorities might change in the next few months, making your relationship ripe for a partnership.

Katniss Syndrome

For those readers who aren't aware, Katniss Everdeen is the main character in the famed Hunger Games series. (Spoiler alert!) In the first book, there is a scene where she is practically dying of hunger hiding behind the house of Peeta Mallark, son of a bread maker. It's pouring rain, and Peeta steps out to throw some of the burnt bread away to the pigs his family keeps. He spots Katniss in the mud, sympathizes with her, and throws a loaf of bread toward her and goes back inside. This loaf of bread saves Katniss and her family from dying that day. Throughout the remainder of the book Katniss feels so indebted to Peeta for saving her life that she feels she has to repay him. So she does everything possible to repay her debt to Peeta by saving his life while they are playing the Hunger Games.

I strongly believe that when you do something nice for someone without asking for anything in return, they're naturally indebted to you in some way and are more likely to follow through when you ask for their help. This is what I call the Katniss Syndrome.

Business relationships are sacred to a lot of people. Many only open up their networks with the intention of immediately asking for something in return. These kinds of transactional experiences don't build genuine relationships. There is a natural power in two people deeply connecting with each other when one helps the other without expecting anything in return. It's similar to how Katniss never forgot that moment Peeta gave her bread; your contact won't forget when you randomly reached out to help her without expecting a thing in return. This will keep you top of mind if the perfect opportunity comes up for you.

Tweetable Takeaway

Share your resources with those you value without expecting anything in return.

Show Up

Woody Allen famously said, "Showing up is 80 percent of life. Sometimes it's easier to hide home in bed." When your partners invite you to an event, GO. It's as simple as that. They invited you into their network because they like you, want you to be in the company of their peers, and value your presence. The more you show up and create shared experiences, the deeper your relationship becomes. Out-of-work events are a great way to build rapport with partners who tend to keep work and life separate. A few drinks or a few good friends always loosen people up a little.

Most important, showing up is about showing your support. There are times in every partnership that you want your partners to show up for you in the form of turning something around at the last minute, doing you a favor, or changing expectations. You need to do the same by supporting them in their endeavors. Plus, nobody likes to be stood up.

Define Clear Roles between Partners

Negotiations are at the heart of good relationships. It's incredibly important to understand your partner's needs (business and other-wise), values (personal and professional), and program expectations. Identifying these should almost always be an explicit conversation between all stakeholders of the partnership before signing an agreement. At DoSomething.org, we have a one-sheet that includes basic questions that help us determine our partners' expectations. We work with our Data team to figure out what realistic participant and impact goals are, our Marketing team identifies relevant marketing partners and the media impressions we aim to get, and our Campaigns team puts a broad timeline together that details how the program will be executed week by week. We review all of this with the partner on our partnership kickoff call to make sure we're all on the same page. By the end of this call, we have clear goals and expectations that we summarize in an e-mail and share with all stakeholders.

This written summary comes in handy when (1) the partner wants more things than you both originally agreed to, and (2) you want to do a pulse check during the program to see if you're meeting your goals or not. This summary can be bulleted into a partnership agreement or a stand-alone addendum with more details than you'd want to include in a legal document.

Tweetable Takeaway

Clearly define roles and expectations at the beginning of a partnership. If issues arise, you can refer back to what you both agreed to.

Who takes the lead during this conversation? There can only be one Queen Bee (QB)—and it's almost always the organization running the program. It should be clear to your partners that they are working with you because you are the expert in your space. You do this by actually leading. Don't wait for your partners to initiate a follow-up call; e-mail them a few dates. Don't wait for your partners to set the agenda for your next meeting; write it and ask for feedback. Don't wait for your partners to offer ideas; come with your own ideas and invite them to build on them. Your role is to facilitate the conversation so that you are able to get as much support as you need to successfully execute your program—and so that your partners feel valued and included in every step of the process even though you are steering the ship.

> ### Tweetable Takeaway
> Take the lead. Be prepared, open, and always invite conversation before making any big decisions that could affect the program.

Remember That It's OK to Say No Sometimes

As much as we'd like to, we cannot take on every project that comes our way. Money is not worth compromising your purpose or your staff. Years ago when DoSomething.org was going broke with a failing business model, a big partner offered us almost $400,000 to start DS chapters across the country. They wanted these chapters to be in towns where the company had local offices. Strategically this just didn't make sense for us, because we were about to become an exclusively online platform for young people. Even though that amount of money would have pulled us out of the red, it would not have helped sustain us in the long term. So we said no.

Another partner was a great strategic partner for a campaign on bullying, but was a roadblock on many decisions that limited the campaign's reach and impact. Our organization's goal is to make each campaign as big and as impactful as possible; so if a partner is hindering that in any way, it's clear we're driving toward different destinations. We thanked them for their support and with the utmost respect did not ask them to work with us on that campaign again.

We hear so many horror stories of the terrible way organizations allow themselves to be treated just because it's convenient for the funder. At DoSomething.org we don't give it all up for money. This sends a clear message to the Business Development team to find partners who trust our expertise, will allow us to do what we're great at, and see us as equal partners.

Tweetable Takeaway

If a partner doesn't fit your culture, values, or vision, end the partnership—not the relationship.

But It's ALWAYS Necessary to Say Thank You

When was the last time you received a handwritten thank-you note or even a thank-you phone call? An e-mail is nice, of course, but it's predictable and easy. Receiving a thank-you note when it's unexpected makes a real impression. It feels personal and heartfelt—because it is. We write thank-you notes for all sorts of things: an awesome tweet, a great article, a helpful conversation . . . not just a donation. When someone takes the time to help you, you need to return some time to acknowledge that support.

The substance of a thank-you note is also important. If someone made an introduction, let the connector know what exciting new thing happened as a result of his generosity. If someone suggested a new approach to a problem, tell her how it evolved the system.

Notes and calls are sweet gestures, but there are many different ways to show your appreciation. Thank-you gifts can be fun (like the time someone gave Nancy a pair of Hello Kitty roller skates—because she's obsessed with Hello Kitty and they move quickly like her). Or the time we sent an Elvis impersonator singing telegram to a funder. Creativity matters—because it says you cared enough to think of something original.

YOUR VALUE TO PARTNERS

So why would someone want to work with a not-for-profit? Well, not-for-profit doesn't mean no profit. Not-for-profits do make a profit via funds we receive from corporate partnerships. We just invest it all back into the organization. Identifying the value your organization offers is incredibly important in ensuring that you maintain your competitive advantage when looking for partners. Corporate and foundation partners meet with hundreds of organizations. Why is yours different? What unique asset do you bring to the table? Are you more fun, do you have a unique model or platform, a better network, expertise, a big audience? Find your edge and work it to your advantage.

DoSomething.org offers access to a host of marketing, social media, celebrity, tech, and data opportunities that keep partners coming back for more. We can talk for pages on the topic, so let's break it down simply. We want every one of our partnerships to be fun and supportive, not just utilitarian. That's why we share our expertise and open up our network to partners while maintaining the right mixture of spice, fun, and TLC. These are just some of the perks we give our partners.

Share Your Knowledge

Sharing your internal knowledge shows your partners and the world that you're an influencer, a leader in the space—not just an org to make a donation to. For DoSomething.org, that is the bulk of what we offer— our "teen-knowing muscle." Meet TMI. The TMI Agency is our newest addition to the DoSomething.org family. It is a subsidiary agency (also a not-for-profit) created to bottle up all the interior knowledge our team has and share it with the world—it's called TMI, an acronym for "too much information," for this reason. TMI's competitive advantage is that all of our knowledge comes from doing. For example, we know mobile not because we research it, but because we text with (not just to; there is a difference) over two million young people every week. We know what resonates with teens and what doesn't based on our own history of testing new ideas. We know we have incredibly valuable information that will benefit organizations and companies trying to do good. Why hoard this data when it can become a separate funding stream for DoSomething.org and help more people do more good by making the best, data-informed decisions?

Basically, we take care of all the messy research to find insights that help our partners make the best possible program for young people. This is what agile NPOs do: see a problem and fix it. We saw a need for a solid source of teen expertise, and we offered it to the world in the shape of a not-for-profit marketing agency.

Think about your own organization:

- What is your specialty?
- Has your work made you an informed expert in a topic?
- How can you share this knowledge with the world (for a profit, or not)?
- Why is this knowledge a benefit to future partners or supporters?
- What unique assets does each of your organization's teams bring to a partnership?

Share Your Network

Introducing your partners to your network can do wonders for the relationship. Each partner brings something unique to the partnership, which can attract many different people that your partner may not know yet. Show them off to a new or even potential partner to let them see the company they'll keep by working with you.

Too many companies keep partners apart from each other out of fear. There is no use worrying that your partners will like each other more than they like you. And even if they do, there's nothing wrong with introducing two people who just click. Not introducing them is a missed opportunity not only to strengthen your relationship with your partners, but also to grow your organization's network. Plus, you may discover more ways for everyone to work together.

DoSomething.org often hosts events where we invite all our corporate and strategic partners. We make an effort to recognize the synergies between partners and introduce them to each other. Aside from it just being a nice thing to do, one door opened opens another. Each time we've introduced our partners to each other, and sometimes even to other NPOs, our relationship, DoSomething.org's clout, and our personal network have strengthened. There are two especially fun events that exemplify this: the Annual Meeting and the DoSomething.org Upfront.

An annual meeting may sound like the most boring event possible. It's actually a blast. We bring in leading experts and figureheads from the teen space, such as author Seth Godin, and panelists from everywhere from BuzzFeed to Pew Research to *Seventeen*. The day is an opportunity to be completely transparent about our financials, successes, failures, and big plans for the coming year to all our stakeholders and DS fans. The audience is packed with corporate and marketing partners, leaders from other orgs, and pretty much anyone interested in young people and social change. People network during the break while enjoying a full hot chocolate bar and post-meeting cocktail hour. It's an incredible way to open our network to one another and to a lot of young social entrepreneurs who could only benefit by meeting corporate leaders who care about social change.

Our second event is the DoSomething.org Upfront, a two-hour breakfast presentation open to corporate partners and marketing professionals. Our Campaigns team highlights past campaigns' success, publicly celebrates any partners present, and discusses campaigns that are coming up (especially unsponsored ones, in case someone in the room can open a door for us). Our Data team reveals new information they've been gathering over the past six months about trends in youth culture and their experience with causes and social change. While this might sound pretty tedious for an 8 A.M. event, we make it fun. Our first Upfront celebrated the joys of eating bacon and the sexiness that is Ryan Gosling. Our second was planned for the morning of Halloween, so it was a costume party. And, much to our surprise, more than half the audience actually wore costumes.

These events are an opportunity for us to show off all the awesome people we're lucky to be surrounded by, as well as an expression of the DoSomething.org brand and what people expect from us: we make boring meetings fun. They offer information valuable to the audience

regardless of whether they work with us directly or not. And promote a culture of transparency that builds our credibility.

Tweetable Takeaway

Events should make your partners feel like they're part of the entire organization, not just the program they support.

When introducing partners to your network, try considering:

- What relationships do you have that could benefit both parties?
- What opportunities do you give your network to meet each other?
- How might your existing network come together for a common goal?

Take note of fun and creative events you hear about or attend—they may be an opportunity for your network as well.

Keep It Fresh

It's not just things like knowledge and network that bring value to a partnership. The care and time you put into helping a relationship thrive make a huge difference. A large piece of this is keeping the relationship fresh and continuously improving.

Clothing retailer Aéropostale's partnership with our Teens for Jeans campaign is the longest relationship we've been in. Our love story started when we found out that the number one thing homeless youth ask for when they get to a shelter is a pair of jeans. So together, we decided to run the country's largest jean drive. Who doesn't have a pair of gently worn jeans in their closet? We asked young people to run jean drives in their schools and drop them off at their local Aero store. In 2013 alone, Teens for Jeans collected over nine hundred thousand pairs of jeans. The store has supported the campaign for seven years (that's longer than some marriages). And, as in any long-term relationship, you have to keep the spark alive. Each year we aim to go bigger by exploring new ways to collect more jeans, reach more teens, be in more schools, and reach more shelters. All this continuous growth requires a ton of ideas and an internal team that feels comfortable sharing any whacky idea.

Our weekly Innovation Meeting serves as a hub for thinking big, loud, and easy. We live by the phrase "the best ideas aren't in the room" which is why, for example, we appreciate if someone on the Tech team has a marketing idea or if an intern can give us a brilliant campaign idea. Cross-departmental collaboration happens often and these meetings encourage it. Anyone can present a new idea that either gets "shipped" or sent back to be reformulated based on new feedback. Often, these meetings lead to new experiments that inform a lot of our strategy. Presentations are also about new approaches to incentives, PSA concepts, campaign formats, and beyond. We try to keep our presentations short with plenty of time for debate, discussion, and feedback. And everyone is invited to weigh in, from our young interns to even some office guests who have joined in on these meetings.

In addition to keeping the program fresh, you've got to keep the relationship fresh. And, sometimes it just goes back to showing the other person that you care. We make sure that when someone is awesome, they know they are awesome. For example, we use the Do Something Awards to give our top five young entrepreneurs a gold flying sneaker trophy. This same trophy is also given to companies that share our passion and excitement for growing an army of teens who want to change the world. It is a physical reminder to our supporters that we value them as part of the DoSomething.org family. We also make a point to remember birthdays, support new ventures, and send a smile on a bad day. Not because we want something, but because we actually care.

Consider the following when reflecting on existing relationships:

- Does your team take time to evaluate how a partnership is growing and improving?
- Do you have a culture that allows any staff member (or intern or visitor) to give feedback and suggestions—no matter how wacky?
- How do you make sure your partners know you care about them?

Keep It Fun

Providing value to your partners doesn't have to be serious all the time. We look at every moment together as a time to laugh, enjoy, and learn from each other. The Social Good Cage Match is an example of one of these times. Last fall, we transformed our office into a rowdy boxing ring—sassy referee included. Instead of throwing punches, we had experts from the not-for-profit space tag-team debate on some of the industry's toughest questions. Popcorn throwing and heckling were

encouraged while enjoying local brew. Each pair had one minute to collectively respond to a question—and only fifteen minutes to prepare. In the final round, both teams competed on the fly. The cage match brought people from the for-profit and not-for-profit space together to boost their knowledge about today's social problems, to debate, and to laugh together—something the two sectors don't often do in the same room. It even cultivated new partnerships and inspired events that have kept the social change community alive.

The gifts and invitations to unique events are perks of being a part of the DoSomething.org family. These are not strategic moves we're making on a chessboard. We genuinely love our partners and love having fun. It's what our company culture demands. We aren't suggesting that a Social Good Cage Match is for every office, but we are suggesting that you consider how to bring some lightheartedness to your relationships. You can start by asking yourself:

- What are the unique aspects of your company culture that you could share with your partners?
- What makes you and your team smile? Chances are your partners will appreciate it too.
- Get your team to brainstorm fun ideas that show your partners you care and that reflect your brand and your voice.

Offer Some TLC

Any healthy relationship thrives on the sense of companionship you cultivate. One of the best parts of DoSomething.org is the young, creative,
and passionate people that make it all happen.

When the organization was founded twenty years ago, the majority
of our current staff wasn't even through the first grade. That youthful
energy and passion define who we are and is reflected in our day-to-day
life through our open office space, karaoke nights, popcorn machine,
bake-offs, and staff meetings that turn into a cause-y version of TMZ.
This culture is then reflected in our whacky marketing ideas (Google
"Stamos Day DoSomething.org"), how we analyze our data, our PSAs—
everything. Plus, our team is constantly up on the latest apps, blogs,
celeb crushes, and gossip needed to stay relevant with our audience. And
it all comes naturally and is a great benefit to the work we do and our
partners who support us.

We have provided a much-needed break from the corporate grind for
many of our partners. We have been known to do a few flash mobs or
hop on the latest video trends (search "dosomething.org harlem shake").
Our Business Development and Marketing teams often find unique
ways to say thank you or congratulations to our partners.

We have sent everything from fifty pieces of bacon for a fiftieth
birthday to a Michael Jackson impersonator.

Tweetable Takeaway

When showing people you care, do something unexpected that shows you pay attention to what makes them "them."

Perks also don't have to cost anything; it's actually better if they don't. Introducing someone to a new contact (as discussed earlier), acknowledging a partner in an interview with a national newspaper, and inviting an associate to speak on a panel with you are all free but go a long way.

Think about your partners' needs and their goals. Helping them achieve their goals should be a goal of yours as well. Here are some things to think about:

- When are your partners' birthdays?
- Take note of big life events (promotion, a new baby, and so on).
- The little things (they may love mint Oreos or may have an obsession with a certain author or a major celebrity crush) are important too.

- How can you bring the community you work with together? Is it an event? Publication? Forum?

Can We Talk?

It would be ideal for all partnerships to run without a hitch; but no matter how the great people, there may still be bumps in the road. Whether it's the process of re-signing a partner, bringing on new ones, confronting a problem, or ending a relationship, you have to handle each situation with care.

RE-SIGNING A PARTNER

The goal of any great first date is to land a second one. We know we've really blown them away when we make it to the second date. The same rule applies here: one of the biggest indications of a successful organization is the number of repeat partners it has. Re-signing a current partner is much easier than landing a new one. And long-term partners often contribute a lot more to the partnership as years go by, leading to better and bigger programs.

Trying to re-sign a partner year after year is a lot of work. If year one was a success, how do we turn that partnership into a multiyear agreement? Most organizations' programs are annually consistent, and thus it makes sense to build a relationship with a partner that will help invest, improve, and scale the program each year. The key here is to show measurable growth, make it clear what assets you bring to the table (and will in the future), and achieve a data-informed vision of the ROI for the partner. And, if a multiyear partnership is not possible due to company rules or budgetary restrictions, create a program that a partner feels they own and must support every year.

Re-signing is about harnessing the joy of your current success and making it bigger and better for the future. Let's go back to the Aéropostale Teens for Jeans example, as the relationship is now in its eighth year. It works so well not just because we reach our goals of collecting hundreds of thousands of jeans for homeless youths, but also because we've built incredible trust in each other's ability to make the program bigger and louder each year. Over the last seven years, we've collected over 3.5 million pairs of jeans for homeless youths. This campaign is both impactful and brings young people into Aero stores during January—their slowest month. The campaign has been so successful that we propose to each other and get married every year. Teens for Jeans is as much associated with Aéropostale as it is with DoSomething.org.

In addition to setting expectations at the beginning of the partnership, we always have an honest wrap call with our partners. The goal is to openly discuss whether we achieved the goals we established, what could've been better, and how we envision the following year. Honesty is a feel-good word, but you have to practice it consistently to enjoy the payoff. At DoSomething.org, we are never afraid to be honest with our partners if we know—and can back up with data—that some of their ideas might not be effective. We also expect our partners to be honest with us about the things we could've done better. Once you establish this kind of conversation as a foundation of the relationship, it becomes ingrained as a critical value for the partnership that need not lead to any awkwardness or hurt feelings.

Having a mutually honest relationship as early as possible will make you a better organization to partner with in the future. At the end of each campaign's wrap call, we take note of specific feedback from partners and apply it to our re-signing pitch. We make it clear that we've heard their concerns and found solutions for them to make the next year better. And we share this feedback with our entire team. Often, the feedback we receive doesn't only affect those who worked directly on the particular campaign. This also allows us to design campaigns with partners' priorities in mind.

We know it's not common or easy to give feedback to a funder. But it's crucial that an organization use its expertise to show what the program could look like if we did things differently. This kind of effort can build incredible programs that show the kind of success that neither the partner nor the organization has seen before. It's also about showing our partners that we're able to have difficult conversations to make our partnership successful. If their strategy is proven ineffective, it's our responsibility as experts in the space to give them a heads up in case they're applying the same thinking elsewhere. Thus, this conversation should move beyond feelings and perceptions and look instead at what the data and hard facts say.

Of course, you also want to have honest conversations about things that have gone well. Celebrating the contributions of a partner in the program's success privately (via quick e-mails) or publicly (via social media, a news outlet, or at an industry conference) will win you a ton of kudos as you ready yourself to re-sign them for another year's partnership.

- What do you do to prepare when you re-sign with a partner?
- Consider prepping a final report or presentation illustrating not just the outcomes of the partnership but also the lessons and potential areas for improvement.
- What is your system for handling and implementing feedback?
- Can you offer partners a win/win? What is that edge that will keep them coming back?

HOW TO BRING ON A THIRD PARTNER

Bringing a third party into any duo can be risky. Imagine A-Rod signing to the Yankees—and then signing to the Mets. It just wouldn't work. But signing with the Yankees and contracting a world-class batting coach would be a win for everyone. On the one hand, if all parties benefit each other and are working toward a common goal, a three-way partnership can absolutely work. On the other hand, it can seriously mess up a great relationship if carried out without ultimate transparency for all involved.

There are a few ways to really make this type of relationship click so that every partner feels valued with an equal stake in success. Clearly defining the two relationships with specific titles (e.g., "corporate partner," "strategic partner," "organizational supporter") will set realistic expectations for everyone. Similarly, defining each partner's role in the partnership will avoid any future drama if one gets more public attention than the other.

Foundations are generally extremely excited to have other partners on board, as they have less of an investment in brand identity and marketing. On the other side of the spectrum, corporate partners don't like sharing their investment in a program; they worry it will dilute their brand awareness. If multiple partners are supporting a program, you must make it clear from the beginning what role each company or organization plays and what priority each receives when it comes to media recognition. After defining these titles, each partner should sign off on their list of responsibilities as well as the specific items they should expect to receive from you.

If each party can follow clearly defined purposes, the relationship can become symbiotic. The partners must each know why they are special, and why their role is needed and important in the program's success. Praising each partner's contribution to the program in front of both partners is a great way to celebrate them and reiterate what their roles are.

Finally, establish expectations early on for approvals, involvement in decision making, and so forth. More often than not, monetary support buys a partner added say in the process. If two partners contributed equally to the program, it's obvious everyone has an equal say in all aspects of the program. In the case where a strategic partner (an org or marketing channel that gives pro bono service in return for a stake in the program) is invited in addition to a primary partner, roles need to be carefully defined. Make sure your strategic partners understand the parts they have a hand in.

An example of this is our Love Letters campaign, which asks teens to create handmade Valentine's Day cards for senior citizens suffering from depression and isolation. AARP's Mentor Up program and Meals on Wheels are both crucial partners in the campaign. Though both brands appear on the website and in press releases, their purposes are very clearly indicated internally and externally. Mentor Up is the campaign's corporate partner, which means they monetarily supported it and also had a hand in each step of the development process. Meals on Wheels is a supporter; their role is to receive the Valentine's Day cards from our members and distribute them to their clients during normal meal deliveries. Although Meals on Wheels has not invested any money in the campaign, they invest their time and energy to make sure their clients get a heartfelt card on Valentine's Day. In order to establish a symbiotic relationship, we made sure that both Mentor Up and Meals on Wheels understood the key role each played in the execution and success of Love Letters.

Tweetable Takeaway

The keys to success in a multi-party partnership are transparency and communication.

Ask yourself:

- What unique asset does each partner bring?
- Does each support the common goal?
- Does each know the other partners?

- Do the partners each understand and agree to the decisions they have a say in?
- Does your org have a clear definition for different partners and their roles in a program?

YOU CAN THROW A BOMB ONLY ONCE

We've all been there: that moment when you realize something in the relationship just isn't working. Your partner is not supporting your work as planned. In fact, they're hurting the program—albeit unintentionally. Your goals have changed, and it's hindering the accomplishment of the vision you created together. Your gut says you have to do something, but you worry that it might ruin the relationship. But if you don't do anything, it might ruin your program. It's very easy for an organization that is receiving money to feel as though they're at the mercy of the donor's agenda. But, remember that it is a partnership and sometimes you have to do the right thing even if it's hard. Therefore, you have one chance to throw a grenade. So, make it smart and think it through.

There are a few important things to consider here:

- Do you have facts to back up your feelings?
- Are you prepared for the chance that the relationship could end?
- Do you have a clear direction for how to remedy the situation?

We don't do it often, but there have been times we were forced to put on the brakes and confront a major issue. You have one chance in any relationship to bring it to a halt and redirect the path. The most important thing is to approach the issue with facts or data to back it up. You never want to throw a bomb purely based on emotion. It is useless to bring up a problem without any idea of how to solve it. This just leaves everyone feeling bitter and defensive. So, be sure to prepare a resolution and offer the remedy while you state your case.

This isn't one of those preachy things that we say but don't do. Just a few months ago, we had a bit of a come-to-Jesus moment with a funder who simply just wasn't living up to their promises. This was affecting relationships with our team as well as the program they funded. It is easy to feel like the funding you receive dominates your organization's health and happiness. But that's truly only one piece of a bigger puzzle that keeps organizations strong. Your team's happiness and the strength and stability of your programs are equally as important.

In this situation, we had a means of comparison that we used to support the dropping of the bomb. Another funder showed us what real love felt like, and we realized it wasn't worth the money to sacrifice our needs. So, what did we do? We told them just that. We explained why this other funder recognized our value, treated us with respect, and gave us opportunities to be better. We used clear examples (including dates, numbers, and names) to illustrate why we were feeling like the forgotten stepchild and how they could help make this better. To our relief, they agreed. They felt that they could have done better, appreciated our honesty, and even acknowledged that more organizations need to be able to have these tough conversations. Why? Because it makes all of us better. This bomb didn't destroy the relationship; rather, it strengthened it, and they have funded us since. The difference now is that we have a stronger relationship built on honesty with the goal of creating the biggest impact in the best way possible—together.

- Are your partners treating you well? Set some guidelines to help you recognize when a relationship is veering off its path.
- Know what you will stand for and what you won't. Then make sure you stick to your guns.
- Build the kind of relationship where difficult conversations like this are possible.
- Have this conversation between senior leadership so that both parties understand the seriousness of the issue.

EVOLVING A PARTNERSHIP

Sometimes really awesome partnerships (or not so awesome ones) end for obvious reasons. Sometimes they end because neither party knows how to explore other possibilities with each other. Each has pigeonholed the other into seeing the other only as a partner for one program. This is usually a result of an organization not doing a good enough job of showing the scope of your work to your partners. Even though your partner is supporting a specific program, it is the organization's responsibility to share all the other great things you are doing and exploring concurrently. This helps to plant seeds that could lead to other opportunities in the future should the existing program end.

If you run a successful program with a partner who clearly loves you, the relationship doesn't have to end. You can use that opportunity to sit down and talk about what else you can do with each other. Uncover the partner's priorities for the remainder of the year, what pain points their team has brought up that you can help with, and share other programs you've started or are thinking about starting. Unless you get it all out in the open, how else will you identify your next venture together?

A great example of evolving a relationship is with one of our biggest partners—Toyota. Toyota supported our anti–texting and driving campaign for two years in a row in partnership with Sprint. That partnership made complete sense: a mobile carrier and a car company join together to stop texting and driving. Our campaign also comple-mented Toyota's existing Toyota Teen Driver program. Over the two years, our relationship grew strong, and our liaison from Toyota, Kelly Fisher, was at almost every event we hosted. We were incredibly proud of our partnership—so we ensured that Kelly and her team were invited to all public and many private events to which DoSomething.org had access. As with many of our partners, we wanted her to experience all of DoSomething and not just some of it.

Kelly checked out all of our campaigns, sent us notes about how obsessed she was with some of them, and often told us how much she respected the way we activate young people to create social change. At the end of our 2013 campaign, she made it clear that Toyota did not want to support the anti–texting and driving campaign again this year because of a shift in priorities. We had a follow-up conversation about what other priorities Toyota cares about and brainstormed various campaigns we can potentially partner with them on again. We both knew that this relationship was too good to just let go. By honestly talking about how we can leverage our assets to create something unique, we were able to identify a really cool campaign that ties together most of Toyota's cause priorities instead of just one. As a result, in the summer of 2014, we ran one of the biggest campaigns of the year with Toyota.

The best lesson to take from this example is that if you enrich a rela-tionship with experiences beyond a specific partnership, it opens up many doors just in case one closes.

IN SUMMARY

Successful organizations recognize the importance of maintaining gen-uine long-lasting relationships with allies of their work.

They recognize that a partnership can benefit everyone involved if both are able to see the relationship beyond money. Each partner brings a unique set of assets to the relationship, and effectively utilizing those assets holds the key to a successful long-term partnership.

Remember, relationships are between people, not just organizations. Finding common ground in and outside your work results in mutually beneficial connections. Create relationships that allow for tough conversations to happen honestly and without any table flipping. Open your network, celebrate your partnership, share your expertise, and make partners feel they're part of your organization. Belonging and feeling connected are two of the most basic human necessities—and business relationships don't have to be void of them. From first meeting to long-term sustainability a few themes repeat: support, respect, appreciation. Keep those in your pocket, always.

QUESTIONS TO GET YOU STARTED:

1. What criteria do you use to identify whether a partner is the right fit for your organization's purpose, value, and audience?

2. What strategies does your development team use to meet prospective partners in a genuine way?

3. How often do you reach out to your active and passive relationships with updates about your org, offers to help, or simply to check in?

4. Does your organization have a clear system that helps all partners understand their roles and expectations?

5. Do you show up for your partners or always expect them to show up for you?

6. What makes you an influencer? What is that special sauce that makes you a leader in your field?

7. How can you bring your networks together? What value can you offer your partners outside your office walls?

8. Do you cultivate open communication in your office? Do your team, interns, and visitors feel free to suggest ideas?

9. How do you make your partners feel special? Have you reached out to them recently not asking for something? Just to say hello or congratulate them on a win?

10. Are there certain things that aren't working in one of your partnerships? Do you have a plan of action to nip the problem in the bud?

11. Have you examined why your past partnerships ended and what you could have done to steer them toward a new venture?

ABOUT THE CONTRIBUTORS

Muneer Panjwani works on the business development team at DoSomething.org managing the organization's biggest corporate partnerships. Prior to DoSomething.org, Muneer was the director of youth programs at the National Conference for Community and Justice, leading programs that helped young people create affirming spaces free from bias and bigotry in their schools. He has worked internationally on projects that empower young people to make the change they wish to see in their community. Born in India, raised in Connecticut, and schooled in Massachusetts, Muneer has finally found his home in New York City.

Liz Eddy is the special project manager at DoSomething.org. She spends her days juggling a multitude of projects including grant writing for both Do Something.org and our sister organization Crisis Text Line. She loves building relationships with people from all walks of life and firmly believes that is how innovation and social change are sparked. She has a BBA from Parsons the New School for Design and spends her free time dreaming up more projects to take on.

—

SEVEN

STRATEGIC PARTNERSHIPS

• • •

FORGING NONMONETARY PARTNERSHIPS

Hilary Gridley, Campaigns Manager: Environment and Animal Welfare

A strategic partnership occurs when two like-minded companies team up on a project or campaign that neither side could pull off on its own. It differs from a monetary partnership because no money is exchanged and from a marketing partnership because it serves as the campaign's foundation rather than its mouthpiece. Strategic partnerships are all about sharing your strengths and buffering your weaknesses. When they are done the right way, everyone wins and accomplishments are magnified.

WHERE TO START

Every strategic partnership must be built on shared passion. Before you even think about proposing a partnership, make sure your target company's values are aligned with those of your own company. The next step is to understand specifically what your organization can offer. "What value do you add?" requires you to have a simple answer to the question, "What are you really good at?"

DoSomething.org's core competency is compelling young people to take action. Our target is young people who have a passing interest in social change but either need an instruction manual or some convincing to actually participate. After twenty-one years of talking to these people, we've learned how to give them what they need. And that's a strength we can offer to other organizations, many of whom struggle to activate demographics that aren't already on board with their mission.

In general, we look for one of three things when deciding with whom to partner:

- Subject expertise
- Ability to motivate a strong tribe in our target demographic
- Synergy of core competency

Occasionally, we'll find partners who fit two or three of these buckets, but we'd rather have three partners who do one thing very well than one partner who tries to do everything and isn't effective at anything.

> ## Tweetable Takeaway
> The first step to building a successful partnership is knowing what one thing your company does best. Only then will you have any leverage.

Subject Expertise Case Study—Cell Phones for Survivors

Anyone familiar with the great work that anti–domestic violence organizations are doing to help survivors knows what a difficult and sensitive issue it is. This is compounded by the fact that you can't control who will visit your campaign, and therefore you must make sure your content is safe and appropriate for victims and serves as a resource for anyone in crisis or currently trapped in a violent relationship. No matter how sensitive you are to these unique issues, it's always best to get expert input.

We heard from thousands of young people who wanted to help survivors of relationship violence, so we knew we had to build a campaign that would let them. But we also wanted to make sure anyone could get involved, not just people who knew somebody whose life has been affected by domestic violence. And, as with all our campaigns, we wanted to make sure the action was both easy enough that anyone could do it and light enough in tone that our members felt good about participating.

The result was Cell Phones for Survivors. We asked young people to collect and send in old cell phones for recycling. The money generated from refurbished phones was then donated to the National Network to End Domestic Violence's (NNEDV) Safety Net program, which educates victims on ways to use technology to help find safety and escape from their abusers.

Partnering with NNEDV made sense; they are out in the field, doing important work that is far outside the scope of DoSomething.org's activities. We knew their Safety Net program would resonate with our audience, because it creates a tight narrative around the action participants are taking and the desired outcome. The funding from refurbished phones helps survivors learn how to use one to protect themselves.

While we were thrilled to help our members support NNEDV, one of the most important aspects of this partnership was their expertise around the issue of domestic violence. An issue so sensitive demands that we consider the likelihood of people's own personal experiences with it. NNEDV was able to provide us with (1) background info to make sure we were not inadvertently triggering survivors, and (2) resources to include on our campaign site for anyone seeking help or wondering whether their current situation qualifies as abuse. It would have been irresponsible to run this campaign without this help.

In addition, they provided validation that the campaign was actually having an impact and changing the lives of real people. Not only is this essential to the campaign's integrity, but it's also vital for following up with everyone who participated to let them know their actions mattered.

Activating Strong Tribes Case Study—Nordstrom and TOMS

Strategic partnerships are not solely for not-for-profits. Nordstrom knows that customers who want to create positive change in the world are a strong part of their demographic, so it made sense for them to partner with TOMS even before the socially aware shoe company became a household name. The department store explains on their website how important their customers' view of social and environmental responsibility is to them and how they sought programs and partnerships to address this.

The partnership between Nordstrom and TOMS goes beyond simple distribution. Stores regularly promote TOMS initiatives such as "One Day without Shoes," encouraging customers to get involved with the cause without asking them for money. By creating events that focus on awareness rather than selling products, Nordstrom can successfully leverage the TOMS tribe of social change advocates to become brand ambassadors for their stores.

Synergy of Core Competency Case Study—Love Letters

At DoSomething.org, activating young people digitally is our bread and butter. But when it comes to on-the-ground execution, we know that we sometimes need help.

The media loves to pit young people against old people. In the Millennial corner, we have narcissism, selfishness, and entitlement. In the boomer corner, we have a lack of empathy, greed, and a history of destruction. Who will win this epic generational battle?

Nobody will—because it doesn't exist. We know that young people and old people get along just fine, because the campaigns that ask our members to reach out to their parents and grandparents to make sure they stay happy and healthy are some of our favorites. Our Love Letters campaign, first described in Chapter Six, only needed two things to make it work: young people who love older people and a way to spread that love.

We had the first one in spades. Our members love making cards, but how were we going to distribute them to their intended recipients?

Fortunately, our partner Mentor Up put us in touch with Meals on Wheels, which delivers well over one million meals to seniors who need them each day. They have local chapters all over the country to help seniors keep their independence and stay in their homes. We all knew right away that it was a match made in heaven.

To participate in the campaign, our members create valentines that include three facts about themselves, in an effort to help the recipient connect with them (believe it or not, a lack of social connections is as comparable a risk factor for early death as smoking fifteen cigarettes a day). They then drop the valentines off at or mail them to the nearest participating Meals on Wheels location, where staff will deliver them along with the meals in the weeks leading up to Valentine's Day. It's one of the most seamless strategic partnerships we've ever had, as it combines our members' enthusiasm for spreading love with Meals on Wheels' well-established infrastructure and Mentor Up's mission to bring together the younger generation's energy and talents to pursue reverse mentoring and community service opportunities that help people fifty and older.

HOW TO REPLICATE THE SUCCESS OF THESE PARTNERSHIPS

It's essential that you have clear goals for a partnership, as these will help you come up with a specific strategy that makes sense for your particular project. Too often, we hear from companies who want to partner with us because "it seems like a good idea" or because "we met at a conference." Neither of these is a good reason to partner. You'll get much further cold calling companies that offer a natural fit than you will with a lucky hookup at one that doesn't align with your goals.

> **Tweetable Takeaway**
> You'll get further cold calling companies that offer a natural fit than you will with a lucky hookup at one that doesn't align with your goals.

First, think about exactly what you want from your partners. Is it their subject expertise? Do you want to tap into their strong tribes? Can they offer logistical support? Even if you want all of the above, focus on your main ask. Next, focus on what you want them to do to reach your goal.

- If you want their expertise, do you want to use their resources on your site, or have them review content?
- Will you want their public sign-off to show others you have consulted experts, or are you basically concerned with getting internal approval?

If you are looking to tap into another organization's strong brand advocates, figure out how they communicate with them. Sign up for their mailing list, follow them on social media, and run your campaign through these lenses. You'll discover areas where you can help them; for instance, if your campaign includes strong visual content, and they don't update their Instagram very often, you can frame your assets as a solution.

If you can't come up with specific things to ask of the organization you're researching, a partnership probably doesn't make a lot of sense.

If you do know exactly what you want from your potential partner, the next step is figuring out what you can offer them. Again, this should be specific and tailored to the organization. We receive many partnership pitches claiming they will help us "get the word out about an upcoming initiative"—yet they fail to mention what that upcoming initiative might be. Why would we want to partner with someone who hasn't done the most basic homework about our organization?

To understand your value to a potential partner, you must understand what makes you unique. Think through the same overarching partnership examples we've noted here—expertise, demographic, and core competency.

Expertise

Maybe your organization excels at research and analysis but struggles to reach a wider audience. You have targeted a couple of groups that share your passion but are less niche or wonky and have a wider following. How can that research help inform the work another organization is doing? Or, maybe you work in the field and can provide insight to a group with a similar mission whose staff spends all day behind desks. Search through everything from their Web content to their media coverage to their staff lists to identify where their authority has gaps that you can fill.

We know our expertise lies in our ability to engage young people in taking action, not in the weeds of the issues we address. So when we approach people we want to work with, we make sure to explain how an engaged core of young "doers" can help the important work they're already doing.

Audience

There are many different ways to think about your audience.

- Scale: How big is it?
- Age: How old are they?
- Income level: How much do they make?
- Engagement: What are they willing to do for you?
- Interests: What topics do they care about?
- Geography: Where do they live? Are they urban, suburban, or rural?
- Loyalty: How much do they care about you?

Offering partners access to your audience is one of the easiest ways to show value—all you need to do is frame it in the terms your partners care about. If you have more Facebook fans than they do, that might be enough to convince them of your worth. If not, what does your audience have that theirs doesn't? And why should they care?

With three million DoSomething.org members, we have numbers on our side. Scale is one selling point for our partners, but another is demographics. Our members are young and enthusiastic, and many of them are still trying to find their main cause. This places them fairly low on the engagement ladder compared to the audiences of many more niche organizations, whose members tend to be well versed in and passionate about their work. That just means that our audience is full of potential brand advocates for any of our partners. There's nothing we love more than a young person taking part in our campaign, falling in love with the issue, and turning into a supporter for organizations that are more deeply rooted in that cause.

Core Competencies

Finally, can you offer logistical support that will enrich the work your potential partner is doing? Examples of this support include:

- Tech platforms
- On-the-ground coordination
- Event execution
- A physical product
- Access to celebrities or politicians

Many of our DoSomething.org campaigns could not exist without this kind of help from our partners. One of our campaigns, Welcome Home, asks our members to create welcome banners for previously homeless young people who are moving into supportive housing. Without a strategic partner, we would have no way of getting these banners into the homes. And without us, the organization Community Solutions, which has helped move a hundred thousand people into supportive housing, would not have the resources to create a large number of banners. But together, we have three million young people who we know love crafting for good and the infrastructure to get these banners where they need to be to turn housing into a home.

Even if your organization doesn't provide such a clear-cut service, there are still plenty of ways you can enrich others' work. Our aluminum recycling campaign, 50 Cans, inspires an insane amount of creativity in our members. The first year we ran it, we were blown away by the photos people sent us of the cans they collected to recycle. They weren't just snapping a photo of the bags of trash they collected; they had arranged them into complex patterns and designs to show off their great work. We wanted to encourage this kind of activity the next year we ran 50 Cans, so we created theme weeks on Instagram and chose a winner each week. For Art Week, our partners at Global Inheritance donated to the winner a recycling bin that had been painted by an artist and displayed at the X Games. This not only gave our members an extra incentive to get artsy with cans; it also brought attention to the very cool work they do.

PITCHING A PARTNERSHIP

After you've done your homework and you know specifically what you want and what you have to offer, it's time to make the partnership happen. Find the best person to reach out to on the company's website or through LinkedIn. If you can't find any contact information, try introducing yourself through Twitter. If you aren't sure who to contact, make your best guess and ask to be connected to the right person before you start pitching.

Once you've reached the right person, it's time to pitch. Focus on what makes your assets unique, what the company has that you want to tap into, and how a partnership will be more than the sum of its parts for both of you.

You want to be as specific as possible and avoid ambiguity about what you are asking or expecting. For instance, if you're looking for more exposure, don't just ask for the company to spread the word about your project; ask for a Facebook post, inclusion in their newsletter, or to add relevant copy to their website. This won't just make things as straightforward as possible; it will also make it easier for the person you are pitching to get internal approval if necessary.

For example, all the environmental and animal welfare partnership pitches at DoSomething.org come to me, so I have to make the first decision about whether to take it to the next step. However, any decisions about social media have to go through our director of digital, while decisions about e-mail content go through our digital engagement manager. This might not be apparent to an outsider, but if they have clearly spelled out what they are looking for out of the partnership, I'll know exactly whom I have to talk to on my team to decide whether to go forward with it. If the person pitching isn't clear about what he or she wants from us, I can't get the approvals very easily—making it more likely that I'll say no.

Once you have caught the right person's interest in exploring a partnership, make sure to clarify each organization's roles. You want to make it as easy as possible for partners by giving them all the information they need while respecting their authority and expertise. So by all means, send over the Twitter language and talking points you've asked them to share, but expect them to tweak it for their audience and give it the appropriate context.

Forging a Partner Agreement

Establishing clear roles and responsibilities as early as possible will help keep the partnership from going sour if there's ever a disagreement down the road. Here is a portion of our partnership template, which outlines not only the specific call to action a partnership is serving but also the responsibilities of each organization.

DoSomething.org is asking young people across the country to [CALL TO ACTION]. [SENTENCE EXPLAINING THE STRATEGIC PARTNER'S INVOLVEMENT.] The campaign will begin [DATE] and end on [DATE], and we reserve the right to extend the campaign for an additional period by providing written (e-mail) notice to Partner.

For the sole purpose of activating young people to change the world, Partner and DoSomething.org agree to the following activities:

Article 1. DoSomething.org will:

- Link to Partner's website on the campaign microsite.
- Write "In partnership with [PARTNER NAME]" at the bottom of the campaign microsite.
- Provide Facebook and Twitter support for the campaign at least once per month through length of campaign, with Partner's preferred social handles tagged.
- DS Facebook: 604,000 likes, DS Twitter: 700,000 followers.
- Provide a final report analyzing the campaign for the strategic partner no more than six weeks after the campaign ends.
- Appoint a point person from DoSomething.org for ongoing insight and support to the Partner team.

Article II. [Organization Name] will:

- Advertise our joint Campaign on their website.
- The site should include Campaign name, description, and the DoSomething.org logo.
- Provide [REQUIRED CAMPAIGN ASSET (e.g., location finder)] to DoSomething.org by [DATE].
- Provide weekly updates on Campaign impact to the DoSomething.org point person.
- Provide social media support once per month on your most engaged outlet.
- Provide at least one [testimonial, picture, quote from staff or beneficiaries] to convey importance of the Campaign by [DATE (before campaign launches)] for inclusion on microsite.
- Provide at least two [testimonials, pictures, quotes from staff or beneficiaries] to convey impact to DoSomething.org's participating members by [DATE (after campaign ends)].
- Appoint a point person from Partner organization for ongoing insight and support to the DoSomething.org team.

WHEN GOOD PARTNERSHIPS GO BAD

Even with clearly outlined roles, sometimes partners have to break up. Just like any relationship, what matters most is that both parties have learned something from the experience.

Sometimes, a partner's criticism can help improve your entire organization. We ran a campaign called Undocumented for a Day to address immigration reform. While it was running, some bloggers noticed that our rules and regulations required the scholarship winner to prove citizenship to qualify for the prize. One of our partners was understandably upset that we hadn't run this aspect of the campaign by them, as it clearly violated the entire spirit of helping undocumented citizens. And they were absolutely right. Because of this oversight, we decided to extend all our scholarship opportunities to all US residents, regardless of their immigration status, and we continue to be as sensitive as possible to the unique obstacles facing our undocumented members.

That being said, it's important to know when to stick to your guns. Our Fed Up campaign helped young people show the world the reality of school nutrition through photos of school lunches. Some of our advisers—who provided invaluable guidance when we were designing the campaign's action guide for students—took issue with the campaign's negative tone. Although we always strive to keep our communication as fun and positive as possible, we knew that softening this particular messaging too much would compromise the campaign's integrity, which relied on students' (occasionally brutal) honesty about the quality of their lunches.

When these issues do arise, a reevaluation of everyone's goals and a willingness to listen and respond openly to criticism and feedback should smooth out the wrinkles.

All's Well That Ends Well

No matter what, the most important step in creating a successful partnership is the follow-up at the end. Always thank your partners for the help and assets they have given you and, of course, share your successes, highlighting the ways their contribution ensured these wins.

YOU ALREADY HAVE THE BEST PARTNER OF ALL

You can search high and low for the perfect strategic partners, but the most valuable ones are right under your nose: your members and customers. You want to see them as true partners so that you're better able to leverage their strengths (and provide value) most efficiently.

Think of our three buckets for strategic partners at DoSomething .org: expertise, audience, competencies. Just as this frame helps us get the most out of our partnerships, they shine light on all the ways you can create feedback loops with your members to keep them engaged while constantly improving your organization.

Tweetable Takeaway
Think about what you need from a partnership. Is this something your customers or members can already provide you with?

Expertise

Nobody has more insight into what your members want than your members. We solicit feedback from our members at every turn. It's important to acknowledge that not everyone wants to give feedback in the same way; think about the different methods you can use to gather both explicit and implicit information. We constantly test e-mail open rates, conversion rates, share rates, and so on, and we tweak the way we show or talk about issues to maximize engagement. But we also recruit small groups of members to provide insight at all stages of the campaign process.

These groups have different criteria depending on what our goals are. Every semester, we have rotating Youth Advisory Councils (YACs) across the different cause spaces. We meet with them regularly so that we're able to keep our pulse on what young people care about at any given time. This is a diverse group of young people that represents a variety of demographics within our age group of thirteen to twenty-five, so we know we're getting as many different viewpoints as possible. We talk with them about what their friends are into, what patterns they see across all the groups at their colleges and high schools—any information we can glean to get a better sense of the overall temperature on different issues. It's not perfect, but it's certainly better than sitting at our desks and guessing about what our members are up to.

In addition to organizing the YACs by cause space, we also seek their help in understanding how we can appeal to new demographics. For instance, we have a substantial number of members who regularly attend and are active in their churches. We know religious youth are very active when it comes to volunteering. So we wondered how to get young people of other faiths as excited about our campaigns as the church-goers. The first step, of course, is talking to them. To this end, we have recently set up a Jewish Youth Advisory Board to help us keep a pulse on the issues that matter most to them, just as we have done successfully with the cause space advisory boards.

Audience

Of course, expertise about an audience is just the first step in actually tapping into that new audience. We want all young people to feel like there's a DoSomething.org campaign that's perfect for them, so we tailor our grassroots outreach to different audiences.

For example, the theme weeks we ran for 50 Cans gave us a unique way to partner with other organizations and media outlets and let us frame the campaign in ways that would appeal to a wide variety of people. Maybe you have a passing interest in the environment, but really love soccer. During 50 Cans sports week, we sent out tips for our members to get their teams involved in recycling and asked them to send us photos of the cans they collected that also showed off their favorite sports. By tailoring each theme week to people's various interests, we leveraged both their enthusiasm for activities other than recycling and also their extended networks.

Competencies

DoSomething.org has about sixty full-time staff that all work out of our New York office, plus a rotating team of about twenty to thirty interns at any given time. So when we need on-the-ground support around the country, we turn to our members. By staying in touch with our interns and YACs, and by engaging our most active users, we have created a fleet of brand advocates that we can always count on to run drives or post flyers or talk to local businesses on our behalf.

These groups are also invaluable because they can test-drive campaigns in their communities before they launch. This allows us to catch and address potential obstacles that we might have missed. Our Don't Be a Sucker campaign, first discussed in Chapter Five, addressed the issue of saving energy in schools. However, when one of the members of the environmental YAC tried to do this at her school, she ran into the administration right away and could not get them to give her permission to bring the campaign into her school. Thanks to her insight, we included tips in the action guide for participating in the campaign if your school won't allow it.

Treat Members Like Partners

Given the great insight and help they're offering you, you want to make sure you're showing your value as well. When we reach out and ask young people to be involved in our campaigns, we don't wait for them to ask, "What's in it for me?" We tell them right off the bat about the scholarships they can win and the cool action kits we'll send to the first thousand who sign up, as well as nonmaterial benefits like being a part of a movement and an easy way to change the things that piss them off.

We make sure they know they can reach out to us with any questions they have along the way. They have our support, but they're smart and they know their communities better than we do. So we grant them the freedom to do something alone or run it with friends, or advertise their drive in whatever manner they think is best.

And of course, because we ask them to follow up with us by sending us photos proving they did the campaign, it's only fair for us to follow up with them after the campaign ends proving their action made a real difference.

Non–member-based companies can apply these principles to the way they treat customers by remembering that people aren't just buying a product, they're buying into a brand. So what else are you giving them? Starbucks and McDonald's promise a consistent experience, whereas Warby Parker and TOMS give their customers a way to make an impact while buying the things they already need.

> **Tweetable Takeaway**
> What are you giving your customers besides the physical product they're buying?

IN SUMMARY

Strategic partnerships should be more than the sum of their parts. Before pitching a partnership, make sure your companies have shared passion and that you have clear goals for what success looks like. Your pitch should include very specific asks and show your value to the other company. "Help us spread awareness" is not a specific ask; "Can you share this grant opportunity for social entrepreneurs in your demographic?" is specific and demonstrates a value to the membership. Know your strengths and your weaknesses and be transparent about them. Listen to criticism, but push back when your shared goals are at stake. Always follow up so that everyone knows what went right and what you can improve on next time.

QUESTIONS TO GET YOU STARTED

Regardless of whether you're a big player in your industry fielding partnership requests all day or a startup looking everywhere for exposure, rethinking your strategic partnerships can have huge payoffs both for you and the organizations you work with. Ask yourself these eleven questions to assess how well you are leveraging your partners.

1. If you could add one new branch to your company or organization that operated flawlessly, what would it specialize in? How would this help your organization? Can you achieve these same results with a partner that does this well?

2. What are your company's or organization's core competencies? How can you lend these out to another organization that does not do this as well?

3. Do you set specific goals when considering a partnership or do you simply hope for vague improvements like "increased brand awareness"?

4. Do you make your asks clear up front when pitching potential partners? Do you make it obvious what you offer in return?

5. What expertise do you have that would be valuable to someone else's project? Or do you need expertise in order to hold authority in the space you are trying to enter?

6. How many different ways do you look at your audience? Do you tend to group them by age, location, or income? What about by engagement (type or level), knowledge, or hobbies?

7. Specifically, what audiences would you love to tap into? If you had access to that audience, would you have something to offer them that they want?

8. What logistical support would enhance your project or ensure its success? What kind of support can you offer?

9. Do you treat your members or customers like partners? Are you effectively tapping into their friends and networks, or does the engagement stop with them?

10. Do you provide incentives to compel your members to stay engaged with you?

11. Do you follow up with all partners to show them how their involvement was crucial to the success of your project?

ABOUT THE CONTRIBUTOR

As the environment campaigns specialist at DoSomething.org, Hilary Gridley runs national cause campaigns from start to finish, from research through ideation, execution, and wrap. Before coming to DoSomething .org, Hilary worked on the marketing team at Ocean Conservancy, where she managed digital partnerships as well as the organization's social media channels, blog, and website. She studied English and environmental science at the University of Virginia. She is a PADI certified scuba instructor and Wilderness First Responder and in her free time she blogs about music for All Things Go and Music For Good.

EIGHT

CREATIVE MARKETING

• • •

FUNCTIONING ON A ZERO-DOLLAR MARKETING BUDGET

Chloe Lee, Marketing Manager and Colleen Wormsley, PR and Talent Relations Associate

Most marketing people complain that their budget is too small. It's true that when times are tough, marketing budgets are the first to be trimmed. So maybe you lose some TV advertising or your digital budget is reduced by half. Still, most companies spend something on marketing, advertising, and PR. If you don't have the millions of dollars allocated for a media budget, don't fret. There are plenty of creative ways to work with the same players and create successful partnerships. This chapter will challenge you to identify your worth and use these traits to construct valuable marketing partnerships that will allow you to hit your goals—with no monetary exchange.

OUR MARKETING PHILOSOPHY

At DoSomething.org, we function on a zero-dollar marketing budget. Sure, it's partially because we are a charity and marketing money is hard to find. But it's also a philosophical choice; we believe that having no money forces you to be creative, as the chapter title explains. It makes you think about how best to use your resources, your network, and your strengths. Want to encourage outside the box thinking? Don't spend money on the box.

TAPPING INTO TRIBES

The next time you're at a family function where there are twelve- to sixteen-year-olds around, hold up photos of a few A-list celebrities of the last generation—i.e., Brad Pitt, Tom Cruise, Julia Roberts, Madonna, and so on. See which of these stars the group of teens can name.

Repeat with photos of Tyler Oakley, SMOSH, Bethany Mota, and Madison Beer. (I know—you're probably reading these names and thinking, "Who are these people?") These people are YouTube celebrities—and they became celebrities because those twelve- to sixteen-year-olds sitting at the kids' table made them famous. Although they might not appear in the tabloids on the newsstand at the grocery store, they have a huge tribe of young people who follow them on social media and will do pretty much anything they say. And they feel incredibly accessible to the teens that follow them.

If we were given the choice to work with Brad Pitt or Tyler Oakley, we'd pick Tyler Oakley. Why? Brad Pitt doesn't tweet, Facebook, Instagram, or YouTube, whereas Tyler Oakley has four million subscribers on YouTube alone. That means he has people who have opted into getting a notification every time he posts something, making him more than just a celebrity or a brand. He is a marketing channel.

DoSomething.org's Grandparents Gone Wired focuses on getting teens to teach older adults in their lives how to use technology like Skype, Facebook, Twitter, YouTube, and Instagram. In 2013, we chose a young YouTube celebrity named Madison Beer to work with us on the campaign—which was effective for a few reasons:

1. Strong tribe. Madison has millions of fans who follow her on various social media, and her engagement score is high. This means that she doesn't just have people following her; they are actively "liking" and sharing the things she says. So when you get Madison, you also get her fan base.

2. Fresh face. Many overexposed celebrities will turn up at the opening of an envelope. The media value of a partnership with that celebrity therefore isn't very high. Madison Beer was a fresh unknown. We were one of the first charitable things she ever did.

3. Brand fit. Madison is a teen who cares about social change. Every week on Twitter she has #MadKindnessMonday where she shows her fans different ways that they can give back. This girl was an ideal brand fit.

Working with Madison is a perfect example of a purposeful relationship. Her strong tribe helped get thousands of young people to sign up for the Grandparents Gone Wired campaign. When time and resources are stretched thin, it's important to make sure your relationships have the potential to make the most impact.

Grow Up with Them

Demi Lovato. Selena Gomez. Miley Cyrus. In addition to being some of 2013's biggest pop stars, they all have one thing in common: they got their start on the Disney Channel when they were kids. And Disney isn't the only company that knows how to spot potential celebrities before they're old enough to drive a car. DoSomething.org has worked with some of the biggest teen personalities before they became household names, including rising stars Cody Simpson and Bella Thorne. Identifying up-and-coming talent reaps several benefits:

1. They're more accessible. The more established a celebrity is, the harder it is to get in touch with the right person (publicist, manager, agent). Many stars are drowning in asks from other brands and organizations, whereas newer stars tend to be more eager to get involved.
2. They have more time. An up-and-coming celebrity can usually devote more time and energy to you. If you need them to come to an event, chances are they can make it.
3. They're in it for the long run. Most celebrities are grateful to the people who helped them get famous. Invest in them when their star is still rising, and they'll remember you when they're big.

Working with both Cody and Bella when they were young helped turn them into DoSomething.org ambassadors. They came back to support multiple campaigns and in turn engaged their tribes each time. Because we invested in them early on, we had the chance to build a real relationship with them.

Tweetable Takeaway
Invest in talent when they're up and coming and they'll remember you when they're big.

The idea of spotting potential, tapping into it, and growing together is not exclusive to celebrities. Learning how to spot a new outlet on the brink of growth has a similar payoff. One great example of this is Her Campus, a website for—and written by—college women around the country. We've worked with them since their infancy because we like their content, their mission, and their team. We share similar goals and target demographics. Because we bought in early, we've had a front-row seat to their community growth.

Today, with over 3 million monthly unique visitors, Her Campus is the number one online and offline community for college women in the country. Her Campus works with top brands but donates home page takeovers, banner ads, and content on their site to our organization through marketing and media partnerships. We've been able to grow up with Her Campus, and they've consistently served as one of our best partnerships.

OUTREACH

Try to think of the last time you got a cold pitch from someone you didn't know. Did it go something like this?

> Step 1: See the e-mail in your inbox and think, "Who is this person?"
> Step 2: Click on e-mail to see if it's important.
> Step 3: Scan e-mail for two seconds, get bored, then delete.

What about the last time you got an e-mail from a good friend?

> Step 1: Wow, I haven't heard from her in forever! I wonder what's up?
> Step 2: Read the entire e-mail.
> Step 3: Respond immediately.

The dream is to always get a response—but it takes some work. You have to build a relationship with someone before approaching with an outstretched hand. Instead of making a direct ask in your initial e-mail, reach out to a potential partner and ask for an introduction meeting.

Think about this as the first date. It's an opportunity to ask questions, learn about one another, and show off a little. It's a firsthand look into how you function that allows both parties to figure out whether or not this partnership makes sense.

While meeting in person is best, we get that schedules and time zones don't always allow for it. These principles still apply for a phone call. You can and should give a window into your culture, values, and processes via the phone. No matter whom you're speaking to, being genuine is critical.

We'll never act like we're in a suit and tie on the other end of the line, because we never will be. People can smell phonies—even through a receiver.

Tweetable Takeaway

Learn at least three things about a potential partner before making an ask.

MAINTENANCE

Think of business contacts like you do friends. You don't just call them when you need something, you don't spend every meeting talking only about yourself, and you make an effort to stay in touch. Invite them to your birthday party (in our case, annual meeting), share big milestones with them (new data sets and impact reports), and acknowledge important things in their lives, too. Connect with them on LinkedIn and congratulate them when they celebrate an anniversary. Have they told you they've been swamped lately because of an upcoming event they're planning? Mark the date in your calendar to ask how things went when it's over. Follow their social media accounts. You're sure to learn more than you expected, and it's helpful to bring up personal information for small talk.

Don't wait until the end of your initiative to share updates; send over a weekly recap of numbers, engagement, and coverage. If cross-promotion was part of your agreement, include screen shots of your tweet, newsletter, and so forth. Let them know that you've seen the work they've been putting in and comment on the pros and the cons.

Once the partnership comes to a close, send them a wrap report that includes numbers about the initiative: press impressions, how much traffic came from their site, and the final impact and participant numbers. Did you reach your goal? Thank them for helping you get there. Partners are humans; they'll be more invested and dedicated when they understand the impact their support has made.

Get their input on how to improve your programs and make your partners feel valuable, because they are! What could you have done better? Do they like the frequency of your check-ins? Was their value clear?

Getting their feedback has dual value: you improve your program, and they feel involved and valued. When a partner feels like they have a stake in your success, they're more likely to champion for you, both within their companies and to their networks. Forming genuine relationships that are mutually beneficial is one of the smartest things you can do to create champions in the right places.

OWNED CHANNELS

Understanding the value we provide allows us to help our partners accomplish their goals, and gives us fuel to create customized partnerships that make sense to both parties.

Organizations often overlook the value of their owned channels—that is, an outlet that you own that you're able to use to get your message across. This might be your social media channels, your e-mail broadcast, mobile broadcast, radio station, blog, website, TV show, store window, packaging, and the like.

Our owned channels serve as one of the biggest value-adds to our partners, because we've figured out how to effectively communicate with our audience of thirteen- to twenty-five-year-olds. We know that each social platform reaches a different segment of our audience, serves a different purpose, and therefore requires unique content and tone. Because each platform has a unique personality, different staff members run many of our social media outlets. The person in charge of our Facebook page is different from the one who handles e-mail, who is different from the person who runs mobile, and so on.

Our members feel more connected to the organization when they expect to receive texts from Alysha every week. They get to know Nancy better through her hilarious and informative tweets. Ben is the guy they count on for receiving weekly updates and upcoming campaigns in their e-mail, while Calvin is the one who will surely brighten your day with inspirational stories or adorable puppy pics on Facebook. And Bryce is the goofball who Snapchats with you to give you a peek at what's going on in the office (including the pranks our staff members play on each other).

No matter the platform, all of your content should be run through this checklist:

1. Consistent. If you're doing your job well, all messaging will be consistent both with your brand and with the platform your audience is seeing it on.
2. Simple. You should be able to skim a post and understand its purpose.
3. Valuable. It should always provide some kind of value to your member or customer. That doesn't necessarily mean monetary value; often an emotional reaction provides more value.
4. Personal. People want to hear from other people, not from brands or robots.

The consistently honest, relatable, and humorous voice we use has allowed us to build a loyal tribe through our social networks. As a result, that tribe listens to us when we tell them about the support our great partners give us. That's a pretty valuable asset for partners who want to reach this demographic.

> **Tweetable Takeaway**
> Owned channels are like different people—each has unique value and personality. Test what works best for each audience and platform.

BE AUTHENTIC

PR, marketing, and advertising are essentially the art of convincing people to like you. You can write lots of e-mail spam or create lots of beautiful, funny ads, but the most effective form of charm is exactly what your mom told you to do to make friends in the first grade: just be yourself.

Real photos are powerful. Not the staged, perfect makeup, perfect lighting stuff you see in magazines, but a shot of someone actually doing something and smiling—convincingly. We've found that photos of our real members taking real action are an incredibly powerful form of authentic advertising.

We received thousands of real-life lunch photos from our members during our Fed Up campaign. They included captions like "mystery meat with a side of gunk," "beige bonanza," and, my personal favorite, "mystery meatball sandwich, old orange, and fish milk." (I'm still not sure what fish milk is.)

Because the photos were original, the captions were funny, and they gave a real, compelling perspective on what young people are being served for lunch, major press outlets like BuzzFeed, USA Today, and NPR covered it.

GIVE THE PRESS WHAT THEY WANT

When touting your organization's accomplishments to members of the media, you have to remember that it's not about you. It's about them— and you are one of hundreds of pitches that they're getting on any given day. Why should they spend their time and energy working on your story? Ask yourself the following questions before you draft a pitch to a journalist:

- Does your story fall under the journalist's beat?
- How are you making his or her job easier?
- Why is what you're doing newsworthy?
- What value does your story bring to that specific outlet?
- Do you have photos, videos, or other assets that help bring your story to life?

You're not always going to get a "yes." So when you do get a "no," make sure you gain something from it. Learn what you could have done better, and keep the conversation going by asking, "Why?"

> **Tweetable Takeaway**
> XYZers see "No" as a starting point. Always follow up with asking, "Why?"

Last year, we ran a campaign with Kiva, a not-for-profit that allows people to give microloans to entrepreneurs across the globe. Because we know that young people are really good at spending money, the campaign allowed them to spend other people's money to fund female entrepreneurs through a text message game. I had pitched a story highlighting a few of the entrepreneurs to a popular online magazine that features inspiring women. The writer was interested after a few e-mail exchanges, but ultimately she passed. It was a pretty big letdown, but I asked for feedback on what type of stories might better resonate with her audience. She told me that she was specifically looking for content that leaves readers feeling empowered and that her beat tends to be a mix of successful working women and women who are working to overcome huge challenges.

By staying in touch and pitching content that was relevant to her, I was able to secure coverage for a campaign that encouraged young people to sign up for the National Bone Marrow Registry by pitching a story from one of our members who had saved the life of a five-year-old girl after she swabbed her cheek and signed up for the registry at her college sorority's drive. I knew what the writer was looking for, and I gave her a valuable story that was interesting to her readers.

SURPRISE AND DELIGHT

DoSomething is built upon the foundation of making the world suck less—not only through tackling larger causes and issues that we care about, but also through simple things like putting a smile on someone's face.

Good companies use surprise and delight frequently. The popular frozen yogurt chain 16 Handles does a great job at this. During the winter months, visits to 16 Handles become less frequent. Through a rewards card program, 16 Handles is able to use tracking and data to boost customer experience and use the rewards card to truly reward. When they see you haven't used your rewards card in a while, they let you know they've missed you by telling you. They'll e-mail you $5 worth of points for your next visit.

Tweetable Takeaway
Surprise your members with a benefit they didn't expect.

If you start looking, you'll see surprise and delight everywhere—from simple coupons, to free dessert on your birthday, to bonuses in video games. They're everywhere and they're effective.

Rewarding people for the great things they've done validates their action and their impact and makes them feel good about taking those actions. Letting them know that you appreciate what they've done in a LOUD way is a great way to celebrate an individual and motivate the audience that witnessed the celebration.

The key is to remain relevant. When we're celebrating one of our members, we think about their experience first. We know that paying for college is the number one pain point for young people. We want to help them with their biggest challenges and reward them for the great work they do in their community. That's why with all of our campaigns we offer a scholarship to participants based on a sweepstakes system.

What are your audience's pain points? What is important to them? There are plenty of resources to find the answers to these questions. Are you running a sweepstakes? Pull a group of your most engaged users and poll them. The power of asking questions and being transparent will allow you to better understand and appreciate your audience.

SUPER USERS

We try to go above and beyond to reward our super users—that is, our biggest fans. You have them too; they're the individuals that constantly use your product, who are repeat customers and brand evangelists.

Super users are invested in your company, and you should be investing in them as well. Their engagement, feedback, and perspective are incredibly important tools. Rewarding them in a public way will keep them engaged and use their experience to draw attention to your brand.

One example of this is when we surprised one of our most dedicated members, Alexandra Cappelini, with a day of social change with celebrity Justin Long. She discovered DoSomething.org after seeing a PSA on TV and visited our site to design her own community project. Alexandra worked with her Girl Scout troop to collect two hundred DVDs, games, and CDs to donate to the pediatric floor at her local hospital.

To reward her for being so active in her community, we wanted to do something great for Alexandra. On November 29, 2011, we went

to Alexandra's school in Brooklyn and, in front of her entire school, surprised her with a day of volunteering with actor Justin Long!

That summer, Alexandra came to DoSomething.org as an intern. She spreads the word about DoSomething.org campaigns to all her friends and even recruited her sister to intern at our office. Now a sophomore at Johns Hopkins University, Alexandra is still one of our most engaged members.

Creating surprise and delight for our super users is one of the ways we celebrate the awesome people in our lives. Take the time to identify these super users and reach out to them. Give them a call to say thanks. Ask them about their experience with your company—the good and the bad. Invite them to the office to get a behind-the-scenes tour. Check in with them regularly and share exciting company updates before they're announced. Grab feedback from them on new products. Be their friend and humanize the brand. By making big splashes in their lives and creating awesome memories, you're creating something for them to talk about with their friends and networks.

IN-HOUSE VERSUS AGENCIES

In 2013, we moved all of our PR in-house. It was a gutsy decision, but one that ultimately improved our relationships with journalists and talent, and that has brought us higher-quality, more meaningful press coverage. Because of our breadth of content and fast pace, we've found that working with an external agency, no matter how wonderful, can end up slowing us down. We're more effective now for a few reasons:

1. Less playing telephone. Everyone remembers playing telephone as a kid. When a message goes through multiple people, its meaning often changes. When a message is coming directly from your organization, you have control.

2. Passion. It's hard to fake passion. No one will have more passion for what your organization does than you do. If you really believe in what you're doing, it's easier to convince other people to care about what you're doing.

3. Real relationships. Bringing PR in-house allows you to form relationships with editors, publicists, managers, and influencers yourself—rather than doing it through someone else. If a publicist has a celebrity looking to get involved in a cause, he or she will call you. If an editor needs advice for a story, he or she knows exactly who to e-mail.

4. No competition. Agencies have multiple clients that they have to juggle. If you bring PR in-house, it's kind of like you're an only child. You get all of the attention.

JUMP ON NEW TRENDS

Teenagers are always among the first to spot new trends. Whether it's fashion, technology, or pop culture, teens make what's hot and what's not, and they change their minds quickly. A prime example of this is the fact that teen fashion retailers change trends about every eight weeks. How do you keep up? In order to jump on trends, you need to do the following:

1. Act fast. The power went out during the Super Bowl XLVII game. Even though the Baltimore Ravens scored the most points, the real winner of the game was Oreo. Their response of "You Can Still Dunk in the Dark" on Twitter generated just as much buzz as the winner of the game because they were fast.

2. Experiment and don't be afraid to fail. New trends are . . . new. Make an informed jump, and if it fails, you'll be one of the first to learn from the mistakes and you'll end up with a great case study.

3. Evaluate. After you put your idea into action, measure it. Data will inform you how to replicate your success or avoid the same failure in the future.

DoSomething.org has gone through a few shifts to adapt to teen culture. Most seventeen-year-olds have a cell phone that basically acts as an extension of their hand. Texting has become one of the most common ways for young people to communicate with their friends. DoSomething.org saw this as an opportunity to engage young people in a way that fits into their lives and began giving them ways to take action via SMS text messaging. Given that teens send, on average, over three thousand text messages each month and text messages have a 97 percent open rate, it's one of the most effective ways to reach young people. Adapting to SMS has allowed DoSomething.org to reach over two million young people in a personal, interactive way.

Teens are also constantly shifting and redefining how they interact with friends on social media. Once known as the social network for young people, Facebook is steadily losing popularity among teens. According to *Forbes*, the average Facebook user is nearly forty—whereas it's estimated that the median age of Snapchat (a social media application that lets you message friends via disappearing photos) users is eighteen. DoSomething.org became one of the first not-for-profits to use Snapchat to engage young people in social action and actually has a full-time staff member (and male model) who responds to users' "snaps" as a way of keeping up a personal conversation. We took advantage of this and created interactive Snapchat stories where we made our "Snapmaster" dress up as Cupid to take advantage of the trend and get young people to sign up for our Valentine's Day campaign.

DoSomething.org is shifting yet again to mobile-first design to keep up with the rise of mobile devices as the primary way that young people are accessing the Internet. By redesigning our site to be more intuitive to young peoples' lives, we're able to pivot and adapt to create the most impact. Adapting is a huge part of our culture, and DoSomething.org will continue to innovate to reach as many young people as possible.

QUESTIONS TO GET YOU STARTED

1. How can you apply a "zero-dollar marketing budget" philosophy?

2. Are your relationships purposeful? What is the purpose or goal of the marketing partnership?

3. Have you grown up with any marketing partners? How can you spot future brand advocates and make them feel appreciated now?

4. What can you do to make friends and supporters?

5. How can you maintain those relationships?

6. What value can you bring to marketing partners?

7. What value do you bring to journalists when telling your story?

8. What can you do to "surprise and delight" both staff members and your target audience to let them know you appreciate them?

9. Can you benefit from bringing PR in-house? How do you tell your story?

10. How are you adapting to new trends?

11. How can you use your resources and creativity to make an impact?

ABOUT THE CONTRIBUTORS

Chloe Lee is a marketing manager at DoSomething.org, where she is responsible for managing strategic and integrated partnerships that help get the word out about the organization's national cause campaigns. Prior to DoSomething.org, Chloe attended Occidental College in Los Angeles, where she studied urban and environmental policy and sociology. Outside of DoSomething.org, Chloe volunteers as a specialist at Crisis Text Line, an organization that serves young people in any type of crisis, by providing them access to free, 24/7 emotional support and information they need via text messaging.

Colleen Wormsley is a marketing associate at DoSomething.org, where she is responsible for PR, media relations, and talent relations to help create buzz and spread the word about DoSomething.org's national cause campaigns. Prior to DoSomething.org, Colleen attended Ithaca College, where she graduated cum laude with a bachelor of science in integrated marketing communications. In her free time, she enjoys running, seeing live theater, and spending time in Central Park.

NINE

ACQUISITION AND ENGAGEMENT

• • •

HOW TO GET AND KEEP MEMBERS

Namita Mody, Campaigns Associate: Poverty, Homelessness, and International and Josh Cusano, Data Scientist

W hat would a leader, company, or association be without followers or customers? Imagine if Martin Luther King, Jr. had delivered his "I Have a Dream" speech at home, in the shower, with nobody listening but a humble bar of soap. What would happen if professional sports were not televised or did not permit fans to attend games? Or, what if the iPhone wasn't available for purchase—it was just a beautifully designed product that sat on a shelf somewhere, collecting dust?

Without followers, there would be no civil rights movement. Without fans, there would be no professional sports. Without customers, there would be no Apple. Simply put, followers matter—a lot.

DoSomething.org is perpetually testing new methods to increase user acquisition and engagement. Effective acquisition focuses on creating and communicating a specific call to action with appropriate barriers. Effective engagement stems from understanding users, and effective retention comes from providing continuous value. This chapter will discuss three aspects of member interaction: acquisition, engagement, and retention.

ACQUISITION

There are three steps involved in acquiring users:

1. Gain a clear understanding of your target market and their pain points as they relate to your purpose.
2. Create a clear solution (or solutions) that address their pain points.

3. Communicate the created solution simply and effectively.
4. (You said three?! I know, I know. I lied.) Evaluate what was correct and incorrect about your understanding of your target market, your solution, and your communication tactics and iterate, iterate, iterate.

UNDERSTAND YOUR TARGET MARKET (AND THEIR PAIN POINTS)

As evidenced by our name, DoSomething.org asks young people to do something—and then they do. You've learned in the previous eight chapters about how they make birthday cards for kids staying in homeless shelters, talk to their friends about texting and driving, give out loans to women in the developing world, collect peanut butter for food banks, and recycle aluminum cans—just to name a few somethings. In the process, we want them to have a great time, tell their friends about the great time (or better yet want to share the great time with their friends), and make a meaningful impact in the cause space. And then, we want them to come back to do all these things again.

Making birthday cards and collecting peanut butter are examples of a "call to action"—the basis of each of DoSomething.org's products (that is, our campaigns). A lot of thought and research goes into writing each of these "calls to action." They require cause specialists to dive into myriad issues within their spaces, distill specific problems, choose one, and then find a proven solution. However, this research would be useless if not guided by the knowledge that we retain and continually accrue about our target market.

Who Is Your Target Market and How Can You Make Things Accessible to Them?

A DoSomething.org member can be anyone between ages thirteen and twenty-five. Of course, we would be very happy to have the entire US population that falls in this age range as members, but since that's unrealistic, we don't target everyone when we create and market campaigns. We do target the majority as we aim for scale (big collective movements) and inclusion (the campaign should be "better together": according to our 2012 Index on Young People and Volunteering, the number-one attribute of a desirable volunteering activity for young people is the ability to do it with friends). To build for scale and inclusion, we work hard to craft something that is truly accessible—campaigns that anyone can take on if they want to, from wherever they are. We also build campaigns for takeoff; once a member finds a DoSomething.org campaign, he or she should be able to read it and run with it, as soon as possible.

> ### Tweetable Takeaway
> Always design with your audience and purpose in mind. Once you're done designing, put what you created back through those filters.

Any age group of people taking action on a spectrum of initiative falls into four categories—presidents, vice presidents, followers, and slackers. The categories might break down something like this:

- Presidents: 10 percent (maaaaaybe)
- Vice presidents: 25 percent
- Followers: 60 percent
- Slackers: 5 percent

Presidents are the minority of people who make things happen no matter what infrastructure is in place (or not in place, for the sake of argument), completely independent of difficulty. This group comprises the minority of young people who come up with the idea to volunteer themselves. However, the majority of volunteers do so because someone invited them (the sender of the invite could be a friend, family member), the ones who might not lead the team to the principal's office to talk about ways to positively change their cafeteria's offerings; however, they'll likely take a picture of their lunch and share their thoughts on it to get the word out about the state of school lunch, as 25,132 young people did as part of our Fed Up campaign.

We try to attract vice presidents and followers to our campaigns by creating an action that either:

- Immediately appeals to teens in all of the first three categories. Something like Birthday Mail, where teens are asked to make birthday cards for the over 1.5 million teens and children who experience homelessness each year, is an example of this.

- Can be completed taking the presidential or the participant route. Comeback Clothes allows young people to recycle old or worn-out clothes to help the planet by running a drive at their school or simply by gathering up their own family's former fashion mistakes.

Beyond acknowledging that they exist as a minority, note the absence of discussing slackers. It's important to acknowledge they exist, but perhaps even more important to realize that they are unreachable—both because they want to be and because trying to reach them would be a poor allocation of resources (they present high barriers and are a small minority).

And to maintain our brand promise of creating opportunities for our presidents, vice presidents, and followers to take meaningful action, we abide by a number of rules and best practices. The three major ones are that a campaign never requires the help of an old person, a car (proximity to home is the second most important attribute for a desirable volunteering activity), or money. Too often, organizations have an age minimum for volunteers; we have an age maximum (being twenty-six makes you an "old person" in the eyes of DoSomething.org). As I mentioned, young people should be able to find an action through us and then move forward with doing it. Broadly, we acknowledge barriers—and then build over, around, and under them.

> **Tweetable Takeaway**
> Acknowledge barriers—and then build over, around, and under the ones worth the creative gymnastics.

Consider Timing

Retailers like Macy's and Bloomingdale's have teams of inventory planners and buyers to strategically decide how much of which style goes where and how frequently based on customer profiles (and customer demand) to maximize profit. For example, strapless bras are first stocked in warm weather "doors" before they're shipped to colder regions like the Northeast. Come holiday season when pajama packs are ordered, flannel is requested for the Northeast and cotton tops and bottoms are routed to the Southeast and Southwest. Sending strapless bras to upstate New York in December would be all sorts of useless. The importance of timing in creating and marketing products is critical.

> **Tweetable Takeaway**
> Timing considerations should encapsulate everything from seasonal changes to life events to preoccupations to time constraints.

Our 2013 PB & Jam Slam focused on a top cause young people care about: hunger. Our members really wanted us to create a campaign around this issue. But instead of the typical canned food or soups, we asked young people to collect peanut butter. It's high in protein, has a long shelf life, and is often requested at food banks. It is also a very specific, very kid-friendly thing; unless they have an allergy to it, most young people love peanut butter and are pretty adamantly Team Crunchy or Team Smooth. This frame elicits an emotional reaction. So, we turned the collection into a competition between #teamcrunchy versus #teamsmooth. Which team would collect more? (Answer: two-thirds Team Smooth.)

Simply, it was a good clear ask addressing a clear problem, with a fun, appealing twist that was relevant to our target market.

So, it was a huge success, right? Wrong.

We ran the campaign from April 1 through May 21. During April and May, young people are prepping for Advanced Placement exams, graduation, and finals—but mostly, they are thinking about prom. Peanut butter isn't at the forefront of their minds when they're stressing over who they'll take to prom and what college they're going to get into. This isn't the time to ask them to take an action that requires a lot of planning and time. The next year we launched the campaign earlier than we had in 2013, giving young people ample lead time to start thinking about and organizing a drive.

It's not enough to simply love and respect your target market. If you want to acquire users, you need to think like users.

We put a lot of effort into thinking like our target market; as such, we have systems that ensure we "fight for the user." To make sure we're not out of touch with them, our User Experience Researcher sends staff-wide monthly e-mails highlighting the latest activities, concerns, frustrations, and preoccupations of our demographic. In January 2014, the e-mail looked like this:

College right now is all about studying (obviously), welcoming back my residents from break (I'm an RA), and making plans for next year (seriously all plans for fall 2015 are made in February).

Junior year is tough. When juggling Varsity Basketball, my DoSomething.org club, and studying, things can get pretty crazy!

Midddtermmmms. (Oy. We feel your pain.)

Because of this insight, we launch and wrap all campaigns with thorough discussions about timing. We consider when:

- Impact will be the highest. We run Thumb Wars, our anti–texting and driving campaign, around Memorial Day because accidents spike during the summer months.
- The marketing team will have a good angle to pitch. We run I <3 Dad, a campaign asking young people take a male figure in their life to get his blood pressure checked, around Father's Day.
- Young people are thinking about a topic and are able to complete the action. We run Prom for All, which asks young people to run a dress drive at their school, when everyone is dress shopping and prepping for prom in late winter or early spring.

Create a Clear Solution

With a clear understanding of your target market and their pain points, you're in a great place to come up with a clear solution to address their problems. A hallmark of a DoSomething.org call to action is its specificity. It centers on a certain issue in a cause space and asks young people to do one thing that our research, existing initiatives, experts, or leading organization in the field has confirmed will have a meaningful impact on the cause space.

For example, we don't ask them to donate "clothing" to youth experiencing homelessness; we ask them to donate jeans, because we know jeans are important to fitting in at school and can be worn multiple days without washing. We don't ask them to volunteer at an animal shelter; we ask them to play with shelter kittens to make them more comfortable with humans and increase their chances of being adopted. We don't ask them to "raise awareness" about the dangers of texting and driving; we ask them to give out a pair of "thumb socks" that literally prevent texting on a touchscreen phone because we know that's an easier way to start an awkward (but incredibly important) conversation.

Specificity is a precursor to contagion; or, said inversely, it's nearly impossible to spread something that is vague. Rainbow Loom is a clear example of the virality of something specific and simple. Though these colored rubber bands can be woven into anything from bracelets (its distinctive claim to fame), small bags, belts, shoelaces, key chains, and—for a very serious lack of a better word—doohickeys, the product is incredibly basic and straightforward. Inventor Cheong Choon Ng created the loom concept to impress his daughters, who were making rubber-band bracelets too delicate for his dad fingers. It was his teenage daughter, Teresa, who first suggested that he should make the product available to people outside the family. She planted the seed of manufacturing and selling the product at scale, and Ng's brother suggested the online platform. Perhaps what Teresa saw was the spark potential of the loom: simple and specific in its nature, it had the potential to grab attention in a world where the sheer amount of content is overwhelming and competition for attention is at an all-time high.

This mantra—simple and specific—guides DoSomething.org's campaign process. With a specific call to action, and an associated specific justification for the call to action, you can create something communicable. The marketing team can tell a succinct story about what we are asking teens to do and why it is important. Teens can tell their friends about it, and their friends can tell their friends; a specific request makes for a shorter, tighter story to tell . . . and retell and retell.

> ## Tweetable Takeaway
> Specificity is a precursor to contagion; or, said inversely, it's nearly impossible to spread something that is nebulous.

Specificity also helps people visualize an action. An explicit goal is easier to picture and easier to attain than a nebulous one. If I asked you to donate clothing to homeless youth, you'd probably start mentally rifling through your entire closet to figure out what pieces you'd be willing to part with. Now, if I ask you to donate a pair of jeans, I've narrowed your focus and you're probably thinking about that pair that fits a little tighter after the holidays or the ones you bought when you thought you looked great in acid wash.

According to our research, lack of time is the primary reason young people give for not volunteering. With something specific, mentally digestible, and easy to visualize, your audience can put a starting and ending time constraint on the action and fit it into their lives.

COMMUNICATE EFFECTIVELY

Once we've crafted a campaign, we have to let young people know it exists. And as discussed in Chapter Eight, we do this with a budget of zero—thus, every effort we make needs to be smart and effective.

Tailor Communication to Your User

Just as you would forge a relationship in real life, you can build rapport with your member base by showing them you've listened to what they said. It can be as simple as using their name, or remembering where they're from, or finding out what grabs their attention. We've seen success with using the information our members have given us to tailor communication to segmented populations.

When we launched Birthday Mail in the summer of 2013, we wanted to let our DoSomething.org e-mail list know about it. Given the information that homelessness is particularly prevalent in certain areas, we sent out geographically specific e-mails. We noted to members residing in Georgia, Texas, New York, Florida, and California that their states have high rates of youth homelessness (or homelessness generally in the case of New York) in the body of the e-mail. Compared to the e-mail that went out to the other forty-five states, almost all of the state-customized e-mails saw higher click-through rates; and in the cases of California and Texas, the rate doubled.

Entities such as the Obama campaign and Groupon have also seen success from tailoring communication. The Obama campaign's tests were less about the specific user and focused instead on what worked for a wide swath of users. For example, when the campaign wanted to raise money, they tested combinations of subject lines, body copy, donation request amount, and formatting. Eighteen arrangements were mocked up and sent to a small portion of the millions on the listserv. The subject line "I will be outspent" garnered $2.67 million for the campaign efforts. Had they used the subject line "Change"—the "G" in their version of A/B testing (A/B testing entails making changes [to a version B], testing against the original [A], and then evaluating how the desired outcome of the product changes)—they would have lost out on a ripe $1.8 million.

Similarly (although perhaps less scientifically), Groupon has alighted upon a very specific method to engage their audience of millions with combinations of daily deals—humor. Dentist deals are promoted by positioning a fictional childhood creature as a societal predator ("The Tooth Fairy is a burglarizing fetishist specializing in black-market ivory trade, and she must be stopped. Today's Groupon helps keep teeth in mouths and out of the hands of maniacal, winged phantasms.") and a manicure-and-haircut combo becomes so much more ("Like your music collection or a public reading of your dream journal, a haircut says a lot about you. Control the message with this Groupon.") in the e-mail digest of deals. With churn (the rate at which e-mail subscribers unsubscribe) being of utmost importance to Groupon, they've clearly homed in on an effective strategy.

GO WHERE YOUR USERS ARE

One of the tenets that has helped DoSomething.org grow is a focus on knowing our members holistically, as young people who do things outside of volunteering. Taking into account what is going on in the lives of the people you're targeting is hugely important. We think about members' lives when we craft calls to action.

In 2012, the DoSomething.org data team uncovered the following:

1. For high school students who volunteer, their worries for the future are all about college: getting in, doing well, and most important, paying for it. That's right: more young people worry about paying for college than getting into college. High school students also ranked paying for college as a bigger worry than getting a good job, having enough money, the health of the environment, crime rates in their neighborhood, their personal health, or dying (2012 Index on Young People and Volunteering).
2. Because of this knowledge, one of our lead marketing partners for the past three years has been Fastweb.com—"the nation's

recognized leader in helping students pay for school." Each major campaign that we've run since then has had a scholarship attached to the action we are asking them to take.

3. We go big—and Fastweb claims that "one out of three college-bound seniors" in the United States uses the site. High school seniors (and eager juniors) fall squarely in our thirteen-to-twenty-five-year-old target demographic, and this one partnership helps us tell millions of young people about each of our campaigns. After Google searches and direct traffic, Fastweb .com was the third largest source of traffic to our site during the 2013 calendar year. As a side note, we don't mind that they come to our site for a scholarship opportunity. We just want them to feel they had a meaningful impact on the cause space and to come back for more community service highs after they've completed the action.

4. This tactic of incentivizing your target demographic with items and benefits unrelated to your core offering is not a particularly unusual one. Banks give away water bottles for opening checking accounts, and infomercials offer up other (equally valuable) infomercial products as bonuses for buying magical cleaning wipes at three o'clock in the morning. However, what is significant here is the profound impact that offering someone something important to them can have in the social realm. For example, although existing vaccines could prevent the deaths of two to three million people each year, there are a number of barriers that prevent people from receiving them. In a study that tested incentives in two settings of improved vaccination infrastructures, Innovations for Poverty Action saw a 21.7 percent disparity in the number of children who were fully immunized. The difference? One setting provided lentils and a set of metal meal plates to the parents when the immunization course was fully completed.

Tweetable Takeaway

Know your users outside of browsing your site or selecting your product. Consider what matters to them on a grander level, and leverage it.

LISTEN, UNDERSTAND, AND ITERATE, ITERATE, ITERATE

In the midst of news coverage after a natural disaster, people hunt for a way to help. Somewhat expectedly, in the wake of such disasters (both domestic and international) the Data team noticed spikes in traffic to a page providing tips on how to organize a blood drive.

We also heard a desire to help explicitly from some of our most engaged users. Two days after Typhoon Haiyan hit the Philippines in November 2013, a member of our Youth Advisory Council posted in their Facebook group: "Hi! Just wondering—is DoSomething.org going to have a campaign for the typhoon that hit the Philippines?" Four other members liked the post, another echoed, "If they did, I would definitely participate!" and a sixth chimed in, "Me too!"

In these situations, we did our best to live up to our brand promise and provide members with ways to take action, including spinning up a campaign in less than three days after the 2013 tornadoes in Oklahoma and pushing people to donate to the Red Cross post–Typhoon Haiyan (while fully realizing and acknowledging that we were breaking one of our core tenets, "no money"). Neither "solution" was a good one— spinning up a campaign in 10 percent of the time that it usually takes was an enormous tax on bandwidth, and offering a call to action with a barrier wasn't beneficial impact wise (or brand wise).

During these two disasters, we ran twenty-six massive, infrastructure-heavy, thoughtfully planned out, individually built, and scheduled campaigns. It was hard for us to react and pivot based on current events that pushed change making to the forefront of young people's minds (think acts of gun violence and untimely deaths of public figures)—even though the potential for user acquisition was especially high during these times.

Now, we essentially have a database of evergreen campaigns across all causes and the issues they house and can elevate certain campaigns at times when they are relevant, capitalizing on times of high traffic and specific searches—with a relatively small lift of bandwidth. Capitalization could be as simple as building on the awareness buzz around something planned like World AIDS Day (December 1) and asking people to "update their (Facebook) status" with a message encouraging others to get tested. Or, it might be as timely as letting members know about ways they can help loved ones quit smoking after a well-known actor dies of lung cancer, or giving members a way to thank relief workers deployed after a natural disaster.

Tweetable Takeaway

Listen to your audience and act in the parameters of your purpose, resources, and brand values to create a better product.

To build a following, you have to build for the follower. Decide on your target market, and then learn who they are—both within the context of your XYZ org and independent of it. Create parameters to ensure that you're doing ideation and design with the user in mind, and set up a system of checks and balances to confirm that nothing ships without accounting for the user (and their many facets). Then, once you've thoroughly created your product and it's made its way through the tests, communicate its presence in as deliberate and personalized a means as possible to increase the likelihood that its intended audience will receive it as planned.

Congratulations! You've overcome half the battle. Now that you've reached them . . . you need to engage 'em.

ENGAGEMENT

People frequently use "engagement" as a catchall phrase to describe any interaction that a user has with your product. Don't do this. It is a waste of time and is good way to anchor some or all of your product's performance to something that you cannot improve.

A properly defined engagement metric will (1) measure something important to your organization; (2) have the ability to be improved; and (3) when improved, have a direct impact on one or more of your organization's core goals. Many companies track a plethora of Internet activity, such as views, mouseovers, clicks, or page views, without first determining whether an improvement to these metrics will affect their product or organization.

At DoSomething, we define engagement as a member communicating with us by signing up for a volunteer activity or sending us an SMS message.

This is a good metric because:

1. It's important. We've proven through extensive testing that online sign-ups and communication engender meaningful, even offline, activity. (More on this in a moment.)
2. It can be improved. (More on this in a moment.)
3. Our core goals are directly impacted.

A great example of how these principles were implemented at DoSomething is our evaluation of our SMS games. These games exist solely on a user's mobile phone. They are given a choose-your-own-adventure storyline, where they are offered different key words to choose different paths through a story to teach them about various causes, such as teen pregnancy and bullying intervention, discrimination, and animal cruelty.

An initial question we asked ourselves was: Are these games considered engagement and do they help improve our core goal of defeating apathy by having our members perform meaningful activities? If the answer is negative, should we continue to assign resources to SMS?

To properly test this, we needed to figure out a way to find two very similar groups of users, Group A having played and completed the SMS game, and Group B having not. Then, we could track how users behaved over the next three months and decide if the games had any effect. To minimize noise within these groups, we chose to track two groups of new users that started their DoSomething experience by playing Bully Text, a new game that educated members about the realities of bullying. All of these users were asked to play this game by current DoSomething members, who forwarded the invite over SMS to their friends.

We couldn't just examine users who completed the game, because users who complete are probably already more likely to do more activities. So we came up with two methods that helped improve the completion rate, and we would then apply these methods to one group (Group A in this case) and not the other, and then measure the average improvement of all users in Group A, whether they completed or not.

The final caveat was that the methods we used to improve the completion rate could not cause users to stop playing, because then we would only be left with users that were hardier, and probably more likely to complete anyway. This is called Survivorship Bias. If this sounds confusing, or you want to know more about it, Google "Survivorship Bias."

The first method was to add reminders after twenty-four hours to prompt users who had stopped playing. The hypothesis was that users often stopped playing when they received other messages or were interrupted by another distraction.

The second method was to shorten the sign-up and game instruction process, and get users to take their first choose-your-own-adventure choice earlier. The hypothesis was that users become more invested in the game and are more likely to finish after they make a choice.

We found that when combined, users were over 40 percent more likely to complete the game. We also found that these methods caused almost no opt-out, assuaging our fear of Survivorship Bias.

We found that over three months, users from Group A were twice as likely to go on to do at least one more offline volunteer activity. This conclusively proves that SMS games, primarily SMS game completion, is a valuable engagement metric, because it improves our core goal of more members volunteering. As an aside, we also found that users from Group A shared the games with their friends 18 percent of the time, compared to less than 2 percent of users from Group B.

These results also affected how we structure future SMS games and experiences, and the tests highlighted two interesting factors of engagement:

1. Know your medium. Mobile users are more likely to be distracted. It's important to remind them and keep the experience simple.
2. Choice is important for engagement. Users become more invested in an experience when they are allowed a choice in that experience.

Tweetable Takeaway
Your engagement metric should: (1) be important, (2) be improvable, and (3) have an impact on your organization's core goal(s).

TESTING AND HYPOTHESES

Once you've chosen your engagement metric, the next step is to improve it. As mentioned in the previous example, the best way to improve something is to test it. Testing is critical because it helps you discover what is best for and important to your users, which will help you engage with them better. To start, a good test always has a hypothesis. This means that when you create a new test version of your product, you have a cogent reason for creating that variety. Running myriad tests by haphazardly changing elements of your user's experience may return some results, but rarely produces a sustainable and clear path to improvement. Structuring these tests with some logic and a hypothesis will save time and achieve better results.

An example of haphazard testing is some of the A/B testing used by the Obama campaign. An A/B test is a method of testing where two variations of a Web page or experience are run in tandem against a randomly selected pool of users. One variable is the original, and the other contains your proposed change. You track performance for each variable and see if the changed variation shows any improvement. As an aside, I'm a fan of President Obama and much of the work of his campaign's data science team. I take issue with the following oft-used example.

The Obama campaign's data scientists tried increasing response to campaign e-mails and websites by changing colors, background images, and wording, often without a clear reason why one would work better than the other. In a few articles, interviewed data scientists were surprised that the image and color tests worked, saying "they were shocked ugly and garish headlines proved better." Most did admit that for almost every test, even if there was dramatic improvement, it was rarely sustainable. I personally have never seen a follow-up article that discusses what they learned about their audience from most of these tests, how they used that knowledge to further improve their products and messaging, and if returning user behavior suffered. These temporary spikes in user response are rarely worth it, and most often lead to poor user experience, with long-term negative effects.

Puppies

A great example of how we implemented testing (specifically A/B testing) at DoSomething is the test we ran for Puppy Text. Puppy Text was an SMS game where young people could learn about puppy mills and get tips on helping to prevent animal cruelty. Many of the users signed up to play the game through our website. We wanted to encourage more engagement, and tested a variety of puppy images on the Puppy Text sign-up page. Following are two of the images that we tested—sad puppy and happy.

Which do you think did better?

At DoSomething.org, the prevailing theory about volunteerism is that people volunteer most often when they experience positive emotions versus when they experience negative emotions. That is, people are more likely to volunteer because they feel good when they think about the activity, and not because they feel bad for the subject. Going into the test, I was uncertain about this theory, and in the case of Puppy Text, felt it would not hold true. My hypothesis was that users would be more likely to engage when they saw a sad puppy behind a chain-link fence, as they would feel bad for the puppy and would want to save it.

We tested a few images, with the happy and sad puppy photos being most demonstrative of opposing sides of the happy-sad spectrum. We then divided our Web traffic evenly across these images, and the results ran counter to my expectations. After a statistically significant amount of traffic, 36 percent of users who saw the sad puppy signed up to play the game, whereas 42 percent of the users who saw the happy golden retriever signed up. We tweaked the happy puppy image even further by making the puppy clearer, brighter, and more prominent, and our views-to-signup ratio increased to 49 percent. I rejected my hypothesis (this isn't a hypothesis test in the statistics/null hypothesis sense, it's just a hypothesis), and instead tested in the opposite direction with a lot of success.

QUESTIONS TO GET YOU STARTED:

1. What are your users worried about—and what do they care about outside of what you are offering?

2. What are your users doing when they aren't interacting with your product?

3. Are you asking for something specific that your users can mentally absorb, internalize, and visualize themselves doing?

4. Do you tailor your communication to your users or to what you know your users like?

5. Are you monitoring what current or potential users are looking for and not finding—and then creating something to help them find it?

6. Does your engagement metric matter? Does it address a core goal of your product or organization?

7. If you improve your engagement metric, do you see improvement to another part of your organization?

8. Are you careful to remember that metrics are just metrics and to use common sense?

9. When testing engagement strategies, do you have a hypothesis for why a testing varietal would outperform your baseline?

10. Are you tailoring your strategy to your medium?

11. Are you offering your users choices?

ABOUT THE CONTRIBUTORS

Namita (Nami) Mody is the Poverty, Homelessness, and International campaigns associate at DoSomething.org. In this role, she creates and manages national cause campaigns for young people around issues from chronic homelessness to hunger. In her free time, Nami is an avid runner and hopes to visit as many national parks as possible. She holds a BS in Economics from NYU's Stern School of Business, with a minor in Social Entrepreneurship.

Josh Cusano is a data scientist at DoSomething.org. At DoSomething, this means collecting data to properly track organizational metrics, creating dashboards so that teams can track their projects, and gaining new insights and reinforcing existing strategies through testing and research. Prior to DoSomething, Josh was one of the initial employees at Maxifier, a digital advertising startup, where he did analytical, product, and client-facing work. Josh likes beer and dogs.

INDEX